Can You Not Spend One Hour With Me?

A Deacon's Perspective of the Mass

Deacon Nicholas J. LaDuca, Jr.

To the many priests who have allowed me the privilege of
spending an hour with them in assisting them in offering
the Holy Sacrifice of the Mass

TABLE OF CONTENTS

THE CAST OF THE GREATEST STORY EVER TOLD[1]

The Players
God the Father

The One who is the source and goal of the liturgy.[2] The One to whom all glory and honor is given for eternity. The One who honored His covenant with Adam by sending His only begotten Son to become man. The One who recognized before all creation His beloved Son to whom He commanded we listen to. The One at whose table there is a place reserved for all who believe in Him. The one to whom the Sacrifice of the Cross was offered for our redemption. The One to whom is offered the same sacrifice, albeit in an unbloody manner through the Holy Sacrifice of the Mass.

God the Son

The One by whom God became man. The One who was able, in His humanity to undertake His passion and death, and on the third day rise again and then ascend into heaven. The One who offered to His Father through the Holy Spirit the perfect and unrepeatable sacrifice.[3] The One who is "glorified in the liturgy."[4] The One who enables us to "eat His flesh" and "drink His blood" sacramentally and mysteriously in the Eucharist[5]. The One who promised to be with us always. [6] The One who returned to His Father to prepare a place for us at His Father's

---

[1] With apologies to the author of the book *The Greatest Story Ever Told*. Doubleday; BCE edition, January 1, 1949.

[2] CCC 1977

[3] Hebrews 10:12

[4] CCC 1084.

[5] Cf John 6:53-58

[6] Matt 28:20.

table.[7] The One, who through the priest, offers the sacrifice of Calvary, which is re-presented in an unbloody manner in the Mass to His Father.

God the Holy Spirit

The One who, through Mary's fiat, enabled the Second Person of the Blessed Trinity to become man in her womb. The One who makes Christ manifest to the faith of the assembly and, in doing so, makes the mystery of Christ present in the Mass.[8] The One through whom Christ offers Himself in the Mass to the Father. The One who manifests the love between the Father and the Son. The One given to us by the Father and the Son through our baptism, enabling us to worthily participate in the sacrifice of the Mass.

The Supporting Cast
The Priest

The one ordained in keeping with Christ's command to do what He did at the Last Supper in memory of Him until He comes again[9], carrying out what He did at the Last Supper through the breaking of the bread and the offering of the chalice. The one, by acting *in persona christi* enables, through the words of consecration, to represent the sacrifice of Calvary, albeit in an unbloody manner, and by doing so transform the bread and wine into the Body, Blood, Soul, and Divinity of Christ.

The Deacon

The one ordained to follow Christ's mandate at the Last Supper and serve those at the Mass as He served His apostles that night.[10] The one, who in the footsteps of his first seven brothers, served at the altar while

---

[7] John 14:3.
[8] CCC 1092.
[9] Luke 22:19
[10] John 13:1-7

the [priests] prayed [the Mass].[11] The Deacon, the one who is called upon to send those at the Mass to follow Christ's mandate to proclaim the Good News and glorify Him by their lives. The one who makes Christ sacramentally present in the world in which he is asked to live his diaconal ministry.

The Acolyte

The one who through their installation, assists the deacon and the priest by their actions as acolytes to prepare the altar and all that will be placed on it so that from it, the sacrifice will be re-presented.

The Lector

The one who, through the reading of the words of anticipation from the Old Testament and words of fulfillment from the New Testament, enable those present to become aware of what they are to receive from the nourishment that will become present on the altar through the words of consecration.

The Congregants

Members of the Body of Christ who come together as the Body of Christ to spend an hour with Him in the holy sacrifice of the Mass. Those who, through their full, active, and conscious participation in the Mass[12], will enable the sacrifice offered by the priest, as well as them, to be acceptable to the Father to whom the Son, through the words of His priest and the power of the Holy Spirit, offers it on their behalf for the whole world. This is the sacrifice by which they will become one with the Body of Christ in the Sacrament of the Eucharist.

---

[11] Acts 6:1-15
[12] Sacrosanctum Concilium No 14.

INTRODUCTION

The genesis of this book can be traced back to my response to a challenge presented to me by my beloved "big brother," Deacon Sam Taub, and the steady encouragement of my "little brother," Deacon Emil Myskowski. That response was to write a book that by right, Deacon Sam should have written. This is a book in which I share my perspective of the diaconate based on my almost forty years of serving Our Lord. In the book, one of the several distinctions I identify as existing between a deacon and priest is their relation to the altar. I note that although a priest takes the altar with him wherever he finds himself, the deacon, on the other hand, needs an altar and must go to wherever it may be found.

In reflecting on that distinction, I came to the realization that a deacon needs an altar from which and to which he will find the graces necessary for his diaconal ministry to be effective. That realization found me looking at just how the deacon's actions at and around the altar relate to his ministry of service to Christ in both the people and priest that he serves when spending "one hour" with Our Lord in the holy sacrifice of the Mass.[13]

From that perspective of my functioning as a deacon at the Mass and its importance, nay, necessity in living my diaconal vocation, I decided to write this book. In doing so, I will share from my perspective as a deacon the actions that take place at the Mass as they relate to *all disciples,* in whatever form their discipleship may take. Starting with the activities each take to prepare for, enter into, listen to the word proclaimed, the sacrifice offered, the communing with the One present in the Eucharist, to the challenge of dismissal. In other words, taking those who choose to spend one hour with Him from their preparation for entering into the Mass to share with Him His experiences, to their going forth from the Mass to live out the experiences that their participation in His hour brought them.

---

[13] La Duca, Nicholas. *Who Do You Say That I Am? A Deacon's Perspective of the Diaconate.* Amazon 2020

From my experiences as a deacon, in serving Him in for and through both the priest and the people, my perspective makes it clear when it comes to understanding why Our Lord challenges us—as He did his disciples at Gethsemane—to spend one hour with Him. But more importantly, by sharing the unique activities of the deacon at the Mass, I believe a better understanding for all Catholics, priests, deacons, religious, and laity as to what is asked of them, here in terms of their proper participation in the Mass, can better be gained. Particularly, this is true regarding why Our Lord is asking us to spend one hour with Him. *Not just any hour, mind you, but the hour preordained.* This is the hour by which He would undo the damage done at the "first hour" by the sin of Adam. For only in recognizing that "every word, and gesture has a history, a significance, a memory"[14] can we understand the significance of the hour by which He would open the gates of heaven. The significance of the hour by which He would provide us the means of salvation which was anticipated at the Last Supper. The hour to be experienced by Him on Calvary. The hour for which He was conceived by the Holy Spirit and born of the Virgin Mary to become man so that in the fullness of His humanity, He could enter into it. *The hour of the cross!* The hour of the crucifixion. The hour of His death.

This is the death that would enable Him to experience the resurrection, by which He conquered death for all time. It is an hour that He is asking not only Peter, James, and John, but you, me, and all Christians, to not only share with Him, but to personally enter into so as to experience His hour as He did.

Yet the question remains: Just what is it that Our Lord is requiring when He asks us if we would spend one hour with Him? Nothing more and yet nothing less, I maintain that this means to participate[15] fully, consciously and actively in His most perfect sacrifice. A sacrifice anticipated at the Last Supper. A sacrifice recognized by Him and His Father in the Garden of Gethsemane. A sacrifice perfectly offered from

---

[14] Lustier, Jean Marie, Cardinal. *The Mass.* Harper and Row, San Francisco, 1987, p. 10

[15] Because we, as Catholics, are challenged to do so by the Church fathers of Vatican Council II.

His cross. A sacrifice so completely re-presented at every valid offering of the holy sacrifice of the Mass.

In other words, this is the hour that you and I, as Catholics, are asked to participate in through and in our participation in the holy sacrifice of the Mass. For it is only in light of that hour being not merely reflected, but re-presented in the Mass, that we come to know why He chose to ask us to do so at that time and in that place. I contend, however, that we can only do so by the manner and way in which we choose to enter into His experience of His passion; of His death; and, yes, in doing so, participate in His resurrection and ascension. Because as Father Michael Muller points out to us in his book *The Holy Sacrifice of the Mass*, "[t]o assist at Mass with reverence is not enough; we must also assist with devotion." Why? He goes on to tell us it is because that although "[t]he Mass in itself is indeed always of the same value, whether those who assist at it be devout or undevout… the fruit we derive from [the Mass] is greater or less *according to our disposition (*emphasis added)."[16]

Because as the fathers of the council pointed out, that by our participating "In the earthly Liturgy we take part in a foretaste of that heavenly Liturgy…where Christ is sitting at the right hand of God. We sing a hymn to the Lord's glory with all the warriors of the heavenly army."[17]

Doing this requires a specific focus, a pointed objective: to not only recognize and not only understand, but to see in the experiences of our particular call to discipleship, in whatever form it may take, that by truly participating in the signs and symbols associated with the Mass, we will gain a better understanding of what discipleship entails. This is an experience that we will be able to gain from the influence of His experiences in living His public ministry, particularly in living His paschal mystery as it relates to living our particular call to discipleship. Why is that critical? Because if it is to be of any meaningful value, the Mass isn't merely to be said: it is to be celebrated! Why? Because the Mass, as pointed out by Father Dale Fushek and Dodds, "is an encounter…an encounter with

---

[16] Muller, Michael, Fr. *The Holy Sacrifice of the Mass.* Tan Books Rockford, Illinois, 1992, p 373.

[17] *Sacrosanctum Concilium.*

God-an encounter with Christ."[18] As Fushek and Dodds go on to stress, this encounter is one that is experienced in a way that is not only unique and personal, but is a mystery.[19]

Now, while spending an hour with Him at a holy hour, listening Him speak with us through the words of Scripture, or reflecting on the mysteries of His earthly ministry through the recitation of the Most Holy Rosary are all not only encouraged but applauded, I posit these facets are not the primary objective of His challenge for us to spend one hour with Him. No, I am convinced He had a specific focus, a determined objective and essential undertaking in His request. And that is to reveal to us the meaning of the mystery of that hour which can only be realized by us in the holy sacrifice of Mass.[20] For it is in that liturgy that the whole public worship is performed by the Mystical Body of Jesus Christ, that is, by the Head and His members, where we walk with Him to Golgotha; and it is here that we join with Him in His sufferings; where we wait with Him alongside His mother at His crucifixion; where we anticipate, as did the Magdalene, for the events of Easter Sunday morning to happen, from which we go forth to do as He commands. Our job is to tell the whole world in which we are called to live our discipleship of who He is, what He said, and, most importantly, what He has done out of love for us. How can we do so? By spending one hour with Him in the holy sacrifice of the Mass. Thus, the liturgy belongs to the whole of the Christian people, whose baptism authorizes them to take part in it under the direction of the presidency of the ministerial priesthood. Why is this important?

---

[18] Fushek, Dale Fr, and Dodds, Bill. *Your One-Stop Guide to The Mass.* Servant Publications, Ann Arbor, Michigan, 2000, p.7.

[19] This is a distinction that I believe is best described by Saint Augustine, who uses the words sacramentum and mysterium almost interchangeably; he uses the Latin word *sacramentum* to focus on or refer to the "outward, visible rite or symbol" {while he uses the Greek word mysterium, in referring to the hidden meaning behind those rites and symbols}.

[20] For those who wish to meditate further on the meaning of mystery, I would recommend reading pages 2–7 in Driscoll, Jeremy. OSB *What Happens at Mass.* Gracewing Publishing, 2005.

Because the liturgy of the Mass objectively brings into play all the activities of those who are present, here independent of the of the edification that the participants feel.

Yet it is an hour Our Lord is asking us to spend with Him during which when one observes a *profound mystery*. This is a mystery that is, on the one hand, relatively simple and, on the other hand, a mystery so complex it extends beyond one's ability to fully understand it.[21]

The hour that we are asked to spend with Him is the mystery which is the foundation of why the Church in the Second Vatican Council (hereafter VCII) mandated that the rites [associated with this hour, the mystery, the Mass] "are to be simplified, while at the same time, due care is taken to preserve their substance."[22] Why? So that those asked to spend that hour with Him can fully, actively, and consciously participate in it in a personal, intimate, and, most importantly, meaningful way.[23] Because as Irwin points out, "The revised liturgy was to serve the 'full, conscious, and active participation' that the liturgy by its nature requires."[24]

Yet, as Oury points out, it is an hour, a mystery, whose study can only "lend to better understanding of what is participated in, as it unfolds before our eyes."[25] As he goes on to further point out, "By better understanding this mystery, we will live it better."[26] But one must not lose sight of the fact that this hour, the Mass, this mystery is a living thing ... "[one] which can be understood only through

---

[21] Fushek, Dale Fr, and Dodds, Bill. *Your One-Stop Guide to The Mass.* Servant Publications, Ann Arbor, Michigan, 2000, p. 13.

[22] Likoudis, James, and Whitehead, Kenneth D. *The Pope, The Council, and the Mass: Answers to the Questions the "Traditionalists" Have Asked.* Emmaus Road Steubenville, Ohio, 2003.

[23] Georges. *The Church at Prayer Volume I Principles of the Liturgy.* The Liturgical Press, 1987, pp. 11-13.

[24] Irwin, Kevin W. *Response to 101 Questions on the Mass.* Paulist Press, New York/Mahwah 1999, p. 31.

[25] Oury, Guy, Rev. *The Mass.* Catholic Book Publishing Company, New York 1988, p. 11.

[26] Yet this is a mystery that Father Le Croix cautions is not something to be solved or overcome but rather savored and reverenced (as cited by Charles Pope in "What Does the Christian Tradition mean by the Word Mystery?" January 24, 2017).

participation… ."[27] Why? Because it is an action … "intelligent only to those who really participate in it, and the means of their participation."[28]

Not passively, but proactively. Neither intellectually nor spiritually, but *personally*[29]. Or as put so clearly by the fathers at VCII, in *Sacrosanctum Concilium,* to do so *"fully, conscientiously and actively."* Continuing along those lines, the fathers go on to say doing so "can only occur through *greater education* (emphasis added)." This, in turn, they go on to say, will allow those participating in the Mass to achieve a "greater awareness, a greater knowledge…in order that they might enter more fully into the mysteries celebrated."[30] For "the way we act, the way we participate in the hour, the Mass, enables us to know something of the role we played at Calvary."[31] However, more importantly, this can help us better appreciate the way the Mass can aid us in living our particular call to discipleship.[32]

Following that challenge, I approach the hour (i.e., hereafter as referring to the holy sacrifice of the Mass) Our Lord is asking us to spend with Him by looking at the Mass from its four parts. In doing so, I look at just what the particular challenges to fully, consciously, and actively

[27] Dalmais, Irenee Henri, Gy, Pierre Marie, Jounel, Pierre, and Martimort, Aime Georges. *The Church at Prayer Volume I Principles of the Liturgy.* The Liturgical Press, Collegeville, Minnesota 1987, p. 8.

[28] Eucharistic Prayer I.

[29] The results of which, as pointed out by Father Von Cochem can result in some "77 graces and fruits to be derived from devout attendance at Holy Mass." Cochem, Von, Father. *The Incredible Catholic Mass.* Tan Books, Charlotte, North Carolina, 2012, pp. 61–67.

[30] As pointed out by Nash in quoting Saint John Paul II's encyclical letter *Ecclesia de Eucharistia* (Holy Thursday, 2003) where the Holy Father wonders "whether even the apostles gathered in the Upper Room understood the full meaning of the words spoken by Christ." Nash. *The Biblical Roots of the Mass.* Sophia Institute Press, Manchester, New Hampshire, 2015.

[31] Dalmais, Irenee Henri, Gy, Pierre Marie, Jounel, Pierre, Martimort, and Aime Georges. *The Church at Prayer Volume I Principles of the Liturgy.* The Liturgical Press, 1987, p. 11.

[32] Daniel-Rops, Henri, translated by Alastair Guinan. *This is the Mass.* Hawthorne Books, Inc. New York, 1959, p. 11.

participate involve, here in terms of sharing in His experiences. I will attempt to do so by "drilling down" into the actions associated with each of those four parts.

In Chapter one, I focus on the Introductory Rites, not starting with the entrance procession, but instead with the actions that go into preparing to participate in the Mass. I do so because one does not "begin" to participate in an event, whether the Mass, a sporting event, a work assignment, or whatever at "the bell," so to speak, but in the anticipation and preparation for that particular event. I contend that if one stops and thinks about it, whenever we visit a mall, the dentist, go to work, visit a friend's house, or go to church, our external or visible actions are the same. We prepare to depart, we undertake the journey, we arrive, we participate, we depart, and, eventually, return to where the journey began. Yet in going a step further, I will point out that our intentions, our motivations, our expectations, and our experiences during each of these activities are vastly different, whether in our anticipation of or our realization of what happened. Because I contend this will determine the focus and degree of our full, active, and conscious participation in the Mass. In Chapter two, l take a similar approach in terms of looking at the actions associated with the word proclaimed in the Gospel and shared through the homily, to the profession of our Catholic faith, and the efforts to identify with the prayers of the faithful. Chapter three focuses on all that one is called upon to do in responding to the specific way in which He challenges us to spend one hour with Him. This will take us from the offertory through the final doxology. This will be when coming face to face with the reality of being present at His most perfect, albeit, unbloody sacrifice, which I contend is the most challenging aspect of participating in the Mass, whether priest, deacon, or laity. Chapter four will take us through the Communion Rite, which I believe is the most intimate part of the Mass. For it is here where all who participate are offered the experience of a close, personal, and intimate encounter with the Person of Christ, Who is truly present in His glorified body, blood, soul, and divinity under the sacramental species (whether under one or both forms). Chapter five focuses on how those who have participated in the Mass are challenged to go and not only proclaim the Gospel just heard, but even more significantly, glorifying the Lord by the lives they live outside of the Mass. This can be in the community one lives, the workplace they earn their livelihood, the marketplace they shop, or in the home in which they reside. In Chapter six, I present what I believe to be the challenges (as well as opportunities) to those of us who are willing to respond fully, consciously, and actively to Our Lord and participate in the Mass. In Chapter seven, I reveal what I concluded from looking at the hour He asks us to spend with Him. And in the final chapter, I propose what awaits for those of us after we respond to Him asking us: "Will we not spend one hour with Him?"

Now, to be clear, many books have been written on the Mass over the last two thousand years. These are books written by popes, bishops, priests, and theologians, each with a particular approach to their explanation of the Mass. This is a point made so well by Father Benedict Groeshel, CFR, in his forward to Hahn's book *The Lamb's Supper: The Mass as Heaven and Earth*: "[T]he Mass, or as it's more accurately called in the Eastern Churches, the Divine Liturgy, is so rich a reality that there are as many valid theological approaches to it as there are to the whole mystery of Christ Himself."[33]

Of those books I have read,[34] I found their focus to be on either the Mass's theological understanding, its ecclesiastical purpose, its historical development, its ritual practices, or even its sacramental essence. Some books address the pastoral impact of the Mass as it affects the Church, the Catholic community, one's call to discipleship, and the present environment and its effect on the Church and its disciples. Others focus on the roles and responsibilities of the participants, directly or indirectly expanding on or explaining what VCII promulgated in *Sacrosanctum Concilium*. Few, if any, however—at least from my albeit limited exposure to the vast literature on the Mass available—have focused on the experiences of the participants, whether priest, deacon, or laity, as they participate in the offering of the Holy Sacrifice of the Mass. That is what my objective is in writing this book.

---

[33] Hahn, Scott. *The Lamb's Supper: The Mass as Heaven and Earth*. Doubleday, 1999, p. xii.
[34] See the Selected Bibliography for many excellent examples.

I take up this focus because one can never lose sight of the reality that the very heart and soul of Catholic Christianity is the holy sacrifice of the Mass. Yet it is one of the most mysterious and often misunderstood rituals of human history. Because when you get right down to it, "understanding the Mass is understanding Catholicism."[35] To do so, then, requires we look at the experiences that are offered to the participants in the Mass. As we do so, try and understand what can be, what is, and, yes, what is not experienced by participating in His hour. In other words, the book will not focus on the theological, nor the ecclesiastical underpinning of the Mass. It will look at what I believe Our Lord intended for us when He asked His disciples to spend one hour with Him. This means standing by Him, personally sharing His experiences from His interaction with His Father in Gethsemane, to the meal shared with His apostles in the upper room, to the challenges posited Him along His journey to Calvary, to the offering of Himself on the cross, to His burial, resurrection, and ascension. By doing so, I believe we will see that although that challenge for some will be both a clear and simple one, it will be one that is found to be—sadly, too often for others—as difficult as Our Lord's experience in Gethsemane.

---

[35] *Catholic Mass for Dummies.* Wiley Publishing, Hoboken, New Jersey, 2011, p. 1.

CHAPTER ONE: THE INTRODUCTORY RITES

"The rites that precede the Liturgy of the Word, namely, the Entrance, the Greeting, the Penitential Act, the Kyre, the Gloria in excelsis (*Glory to God in the highest*) and Collect, have the character of a beginning, an introduction, and a preparation. Their purpose is to ensure that the faithful, who come together as one, establish communion and dispose themselves properly to listen to the Word of God and to celebrate the Eucharist worthily."[36]

As the quote above shows, the sole purpose of the Introductory Rites is to gather a people together to "*properly* listen to the Word of God and to celebrate the Eucharist *worthily.*" To understand and, more importantly, participate "properly and worthily" in these actions, that is, the Mass, it is necessary that one looks at not only the purpose for each of these activities, but at the meaning and intent by which we enter into them. This will be the objective of this chapter. To take each of the activities associated with the Introductory Rites and look at them not merely from their liturgical or functional purpose, but from their efforts to enable us to better spend that hour with Him.

No one who is invited or even commanded to attend a function, whether willingly, conditionally, or even through coercion, begins their participation in that function the moment they arrive. The young lady going on that first date thinks long before the date takes place as to what to wear, how to act, and so forth. The young man going off to college thinks about what to bring to the dorm room, what, where, and (sometimes, with too much priority) when the classes he will take are given. The bride and groom do not begin their wedding on the day and time set, but long before.

The examples are myriad, but the point is that the same holds true for the person who goes to Mass to spend an hour with the Lord. Which

---

[36] General instruction of the Roman Missal (GIRM), No. 46. The specific aspects of the Introductory Rites are set forth in the following paragraphs, 47–54.

Mass? What to wear? If in a family, how will everyone get ready? When to leave? What will the parking situation be? These are activities that will impact one's preparing to "properly and worthily" participate in His hour. Yet the time comes. One finds themselves in the church, in the pew, anticipating the rites to begin. And they do! With the entrance rites. Whether accompanied by an antiphon, a song, or even silence, the priest, the deacon, the acolytes, and the readers all process from either the Narthex or the Sacristy to the altar, upon which the sacrifice of the cross, albeit, in an unbloodied manner, will take place[37] Yet Guardini warns us that even then, a "congregation is formed only when those individuals are present ***not only corporally but spiritually*** (stress added)."[38]

ENTRANCE RITES

The liturgical or functional purpose of the Entrance Rites is to get the celebrant and his party, the deacon, the acolytes, and the reader to the altar to begin the Mass in an expeditious and orderly way. But again, many books have been written about these rites, their origin, function, and so forth.[39] To look at these rites from these perspectives is not my primary purpose. My purpose is more in line with that of Walsh, who takes the position that "the purpose of the Entrance Rite is to make a good beginning, to create an atmosphere of celebration, to help those present to become aware of themselves as a parish community of God's people ready and willing to celebrate"[40] that hour with Him. This is a challenge that will encourage us to look at how it is we respond to His asking us to spend one hour with Him.

As the priest processes to the altar, in his role as celebrant—or put ontologically, *in persona christi*—he is challenged to ask himself the

---

[37] The specifics of which will be addressed in detail in Chapter Four.

[38] Guardini, Romano. *Meditations before Mass.* Sophia Institute Press, Manchester, New Hampshire, 1955, p. 11.

[39] Cardinal Wuerl points out that the "procession at the start of the Mass symbolizes our earthly pilgrimage toward heaven." Cardinal Wuerl. *The Mass.* Doubleday, New York, 2011, p. 94

[40] Walsh, Eugene A., S.S. *The Order of the Mass: Guidelines.* Pastoral Arts Associates of North America, Glendale, Arizona, 1979, p. 20.

following: How actively and consciously does he recognize not only who he is, but what he is about to do? How does the deacon, processing along with the priest to the altar of sacrifice, see himself? Does he see himself as merely a participant in the actions of the Mass, or does he recognize that he, like Simon of Cyrene, is not merely a functionary, but acting *in persona christi servitus*, and has the critical task of not merely serving, but actively assisting the celebrant, that is, Christ, to arrive at the altar to offer Himself to the Father through the Holy Spirit as the one and perfect sacrifice? Do the acolytes just accompany the priest and deacon to the altar, or can they recognize that they have a real and important task to see that what was needed for Jesus to get to the altar (Calvary) so that His sacrifice was made available? Does the reader just see themselves as the bearer of the book to be used from the ambo once the Introductory Rites are completed, or does that person recognize that in processing with the book, from which the Word is to be proclaimed, that they are ensuring that the Word will indeed be proclaimed, as promulgated by Pilate, to the whole world, until He comes again in His glory, that He, who is to be crucified was indeed, the King of the Jews!

Yet these are the challenges posed to the members of the processing party. What about those who are in attendance in the pews?[41] Where are they in terms of their active and conscious participation as the party processes to the altar? Do they see themselves as merely spectators, witnessing a series of actions by which the Mass begins? Or do they see themselves as participants. Active, conscious, knowing participants. Do they see themselves participating in the events of that Friday some two thousand years ago? Do they experience what is happening as did those who participated in witnessing the first "entrance rites," from where Jesus took up His cross; walked to His altar (Calvary); offered Himself up freely, unconditionally, and out of love for the many He came to redeem? Do they "walk along" with Him as did the spectators then, merely watching an event? Do they "walk along" with Him as did the Roman soldiers, merely following orders? Do they "walk along" with Him as did the women of Jerusalem, passively anguished by what is

---

[41] One must never lose sight of the reality that those in the processing party represent all of the parishioners in attendance at the Mass.

happening? Do they "walk along" with Him as did Veronica and actively assist Him to undertake His hour? Or do they share with Him His agony, His pain, His abandonment, His ridicule, and, yes, His death in an active, personal, and conscious way, as did His mother, Mary?

In short, as the priest, acting *in persona christi*, along with the deacon, approach the altar, to reverence the site upon which the unbloodied sacrifice will be offered and the fruits of that sacrifice, the resurrection, will be realized, we will find that the challenge to spend one hour with Him has formally begun. The challenge then is for us to look at our actions, particularly as participants in the Mass, and ask ourselves the following: As the processing party approaches the altar, where am I? Was I an active or passive participant? Did I participate in the activities by habit or knowing what it was that was taking place? Was I conscious of my contributions and consent as to what was about to happen? Was I focused or distracted from the experience?[42] Our answers will help us recognize how we are preparing to participate in this hour Our Lord has asked us to spend with Him.

THE SIGN OF THE CROSS

Upon arriving at and reverencing the altar, the priest formally begins the Mass with the Sign of the Cross[43], which Oury points out is a distinctly Christian gesture: "A sign of the Trinity and a sign of redemption as well…as a reminder of our Baptism."[44] In short, it is the most succinct visible synthesis of our Christian faith. A powerful proclamation of just how much God loves us. A factual statement of how much more powerful love is than evil. A visible recognition of the meaning and purpose of the Mass, in that it demonstrates that what is about to occur links

---

[42] I found a good benchmark for assessing where we are during not only this part of the Mass, but the whole Mass, to be the following: Guardini, Romano. *Meditations before Mass.* Sophia Institute Press, Manchester, New Hampshire, 1955.

[43] Trigilio, Jr., John Rev., Brighenti, Kenneth Rev., and Cafone, James Rev. Monsignor. *Catholic Mass for Dummies.* Wiley Publishing, Hoboken, New Jersey, 2011, p. 64.

[44] Oury, Guy, Rev. *The Mass.* Catholic Book Publishing Company, New York, 1988, pp. 47–48.

heaven with earth and is offered for the whole world.[45] The challenge for those who join with the priest in beginning the hour by the **signing of** themselves with the cross is to stop and ponder: How conscious are we of what we are not only doing, not only acknowledging, not only proclaiming, but committing to not only during the Mass, but in leaving the Mass?[46] This is not only in our vertical relationship with the Christ whose sacrifice we will have participated in but, more importantly, with those among whom we live, work, and play.

The challenge to ask ourselves in our signing with the cross is how conscious we are of our baptismal commitment of accepting our cross as we are soon to not only witness, but participate in the re-presentation of the manner in which Jesus accepted His cross.[47]

This is the cross by which He fulfilled the acceptance of His Father's will for Him which He gave Him in Gethsemane in a most complete and perfect way. In the cross, He is asking of us, here through our participation in the Mass, to not merely stand beneath but take that experience with us when the hour is completed.

---

[45] It is interesting to note the evolution of the Sign of the Cross, as pointed out in the instruction of Pope Innocent III (1198–1216) [where he] evidences the traditional practice but also indicates a shift in the Latin Rite practice of the Catholic Church: "The sign of the cross is made with three fingers, because the signing is done together with the invocation of the Trinity. …This is how it is done: from above to below, and from the right to the left, because Christ descended from the heavens to the earth, and from the Jews (right) He passed to the Gentiles (left)." While noting the custom of making the cross from the right to the left shoulder was for both the Western and Eastern Churches, Pope Innocent continued, "Others, however, make the sign of the cross from the left to the right, because from misery (left) we must cross over to glory (right), just as Christ crossed over from death to life, and from Hades to Paradise. [Some priests] do it this way so that they and the people will be signing themselves in the same way. You can easily verify this– picture the priest facing the people for the blessing– when we make the sign of the cross over the people, it is from left to right …." Therefore, about this time, the faithful began to imitate the priest imparting the blessing, going from the left shoulder to the right shoulder with an open hand. Eventually, this practice became the custom for the Western Church. https://catholicstraightanswers.com/what-is-the-origin-of-the-sign-of-the-cross

[46] This challenge will be covered in more detail in Chapter Six.

[47] A subject that I will address in depth in Chapter Three.

THE GREETING

Once the hour begins, the Church, recognizing the magnitude of the experience we are about to enter into, each in our own role, asks of the celebrant in his greeting to not only offer us "The Grace and Peace of Our Lord Jesus Christ, the Love of God and the Communion of the Holy Spirit," but for us to offer it to his spirit as well so that we all can—again in our own assigned roles—worthily participate in the Mass.

Think about that. How powerful. How necessary. Think about the graces Our Lord offers us. The graces both actual, to truly do what is required to spend one hour with Him, as well as sacramental, when He offers us Himself, body, blood, soul and divinity, in the Eucharist. Graces that without which, we will not have all that we need to go forth and share our experiences of the Mass with others. Without His graces, we cannot truly spend that hour with Him. Without His graces, we will not be able to recognize each of our particular important roles in participating in the Mass. Without His graces, we will not be able to experience the love of the Father. The love by which He created us to be who we are. The love by which, at our baptism, He claimed us as His children with whom He is well pleased. The love by which He gave us His only begotten Son so that through His hour, we too can share in the sacrifice of the cross, not merely by historical remembrance, but by actual participation. Then, to remind us that we are members of His body, His Church, and as such, we are offered the communion of the Holy Spirit, by and through which, we, priest, deacon, lector, acolyte, or parishioner, join together not only with Him, but with all those present in the fervent power of His love that will empower us in a way that the experience of the hour will be fully realized.

THE PENETENTIAL RITE

Yet before we can do so, we need to recognize our unworthiness. The unworthiness that derives from our sinfulness, to whatever degree or whatever nature that unworthiness derives from. And the way we are asked to do so is to literally "stand up and be counted" publicly as sinners. Not in any sense of despair, but of hope. Hope in His promise to forgive us who as "confessing" our sins of both commission and omission and asking of our brothers and sisters, as well as the angels and saints in heaven and our Blessed Mother, their support in our petition being genuine.

Why is this necessary? It is not to recognize that we are not perfect—we know that—but to recognize that what we are about to enter into is perfect. And that to experience that perfection, we must rely on the help of others, both in heaven and on earth, through their prayers and intercessions before we can do so fully, actively, and consciously.

THE GLORIA

We must recognize that our participation in His hour cannot be fully realized by our own efforts, but instead (as we recognized in the exchange that occurred between the celebrant and participants) with the support, encouragement, and presence of God in the Trinity. This is why we are asked to proclaim that opportunity by our echoing what the angels proclaimed at the birth of the One whose hour we are about to share in, for the very same reason: *"namely, that God has sent His Son among us born in our same flesh."*[48] And so, whether in song or prose, in the Gloria, we are challenged to give "Glory to God in the highest." Yet it is a song that is meant "to take the focus away from us and to turn it again toward God."[49] Because, by "recounting in the Gloria who God is first, then what He has done for us in taking away our sins, and finally declaring again that He alone is God, we are making a proclamation that God is our God."[50] This is a challenge through which we are given the opportunity to publicly express our "faith and devotion"[51] in the One we come to worship in not only a communal way, but more importantly, in a personal way. It is a challenge that asks of us, in looking at how we respond, particularly in our commitment once the hour is over, to go

---

[48] Wuerl, Donald Cardinal. *The Mass.* Doubleday, New York, 2011, p. 26.
[49] Dubruiel, Michael. *The How-To Book of the Mass.* Our Sunday Visitor, Huntington, Indiana. 2002, p. 64.
[50] Ibid, p. 68.
[51] Eucharistic Prayer I. A subject that will be addressed in more detail below.

forth and not only seek out, but offer "peace to people of good will." Will we have the faith to put ourselves in the fields outside of Bethlehem alongside the shepherds and join them in going to Him, here in a way that enabled them to recognize in the baby who He really is? Will we, in the way we go go to Him in the Eucharist, recognize Him for who He is? And then will we, in the way we proclaim His glory, be able to say that it will encourage others, as the angels encouraged the shepherds that first Christmas day to also seek Him out and give Him praise because of our proclamation? [52] A song so profound that it has been called "a Magnificat of the Church."[53] Because in faith we know that by our participation in His hour, we will be given not only the graces, but the peace by which to do so. The question we must then ask ourselves is not "Can we do so?" but ***"Will we do so?"***

THE COLLECT

The collect, or opening prayer,[54] has been a part of the Mass as early as the third century.[55] It is a prayer whose intent is to gather all—priest, deacon, acolyte, lector, and parishioner, into "one praying congregation."[56] The purpose, as Driscoll points out, "is to '*collect*,' into a few short lines, all the strands of what has taken place so far, as well as all the strands of our many individual thoughts… [It] effectively places us all together

---

[52] Which the Church has sung, "[a]ccording to the ancient chronicles of the Church of Rome, since around AD 128. It was then that Pope Saint Telesphorus decreed 'at the opening of the sacrifice the angelic hymn should be repeated – that is, Glory to God in the Highest!'" Wuerl, Donald Cardinal. *The Mass.* Doubleday, New York, 2011, pp. 106–107.

[53] Lustier, Jean Marie, Cardinal. *The Mass.* Harper and Row, San Francisco, 1987, p. 36

[54] The Latin name for the prayer, as Dubruiel points out, is ***"Collecta,"*** meaning "the collect." In English translations, it is called the "opening prayer." Dubruiel, Michael. *The How-To Book of the Mass.* Our Sunday Visitor, Huntington, Indiana, 2002, p. 73.

[55] Jungmann, Joseph A. S.J. *The Mass of the Roman Rite: Its Origins and Development.* Christian Classics, Inc., Westminster, Maryland, 1992, p. 372.

[56] Howard, Thomas. *If Your Mind Wanders at Mass.* Ignatius Press, San Francisco, 2001, p. 60.

into one succinctly expressed address to God the Father."[57] It is a prayer we must not lose sight of; although it is addressed to the Father, it is done so "in the name of Christ, with whom we pray, by the Spirit, who gives us the strength to do so by realizing it is not only to His Father but our Father."[58]

Now, we come to what I call is the point where we, in faith, are asked to subsume our individualism into the communion of worshipers. An act of faith in His promise that whenever two or more are gathered in His name, He will be there with them.[59] An act of faith that He has not only the power to, but truly *wishes* to answer what Champlin identifies as "all those keenly felt but unspoken petitions" the priest, in his prayer offers up to Him.[60]

In short, what the collect is really proclaiming is that we, who are participants in the Mass, acknowledge that we have arrived at the foot of Calvary. That whether we find ourselves **among** the spectators who were looking on, or the doubtful who would not look beyond the visible activities taking place, or the disciples who chose to stand off to the side, or even standing beside Mary, John, and the other women, we are all about to witness the events of Calvary re-presented. And of import to us who are at the Mass is to recognize that to whichever group we find ourselves most closely identified with will influence what it is we will not only experience but gain from His sacrifice. The *same sacrifice* that will unfold before us. It will dispose us, in listening to what is said in the Liturgy of the Word, to the way we will prepare ourselves to approach the events that will take place in the Liturgy of the Eucharist. It will enable us to understand how it is we find ourselves leaving the "hill of Calvary" or, in other words, leaving the Mass. Will our departure be like

---

[57] Driscoll, Jeremy, OSB. *What Happens at Mass.* Gracewing Publishing, 2005, pp. 27–28.
[58] Trigilio, Jr., John Rev., Brighenti, Kenneth Rev., and Cafone, James Rev. Monsignor. *Catholic Mass for Dummies.* Wiley Publishing, Hoboken, New Jersey, 2011, p. 67.
[59] Matthew 18:20.
[60] Champlin, Joseph M. *The Mystery and Meaning of the Mass.* The Crossword Publishing Company, New York, 1998, p. 51.

the spectators, sensing just another (albeit horrific) event that we had witnessed before and will witness again? Will it be like the disciples, somewhat "let down" that the experience didn't go the way we wanted or expected it to? Or will it be like that of Mary and the Magdalene with steadfast faith; determined hope; and an unyielding love for the One whose sacrifice was just witnessed?

In our "Amen" to the collect, we will learn a good deal as to how "solemn [our] ratification, hearty approval, [and] total commitment to joining in His Sacrifice," the sacrifice of the Mass, we are participating in will be. This is an exercise I believe that will enable us to be better disposed to listening to His Word and experiencing that Word personally in the Eucharist.

CHAPTER TWO: THE LITURGY OF THE WORD

The main part of the Liturgy of the Word is made up of the readings from the Sacred Scripture together, along with the chants occurring between them. As for the homily, the Profession of Faith and the Universal Prayer, they develop and conclude it.[61]

"All scripture is inspired by God and is useful for teaching, for refutation, for correction, and for training in righteousness, so that One who belongs to God may be competent, equipped for every good work."

2 Timothy 3:16-17

"Today, listen to the voice of the Lord: Do not grow stubborn, as your fathers did in the wilderness … ."

Psalm 95 (as set out in the Invitatory of the Divine Office)

We have arrived. We are here, at the hill on which the perfect sacrifice is to be offered for us. We are at the altar, or table on which that same sacrifice is to be re-presented. It is one of the two tables to be found in the sanctuary. Here, we find ourselves at the Table of the Word. Later, we will find ourselves before the Table of the Eucharist.[62] But for now, we will focus on the Table of the Word. Whether we find ourselves as those who were merely "passersby," those then who stood in the shadows of the hill as mere spectators, as those then involved in some way with the events that are to happen on the hill, or even as Mary, John, and the Magdalene standing at the very foot of where the cross is to be raised, we are there. Whatever our inclination and for whatever reason we find ourselves there, we find ourselves awaiting, with various

---

[61] GIRM No 55.

[62] The theme of two, tables is developed by Oury, in quoting Saint Augustine, by which he distinguishes the one as the table of the Word of God, where we are nourished with the doctrine of the Lord and the other the table of the Eucharist, where we receive our food, the bread of life. p. 58.

dispositions, to hear what this Jesus, from His cross, is about to say. The cross by which the Word is preparing to accomplish what His Father has sent Him to do.

We await, joining with those there that day, to hear what the Word is about to not only tell us, but show us; what it is He came to fulfill—the message given by His Father to His chosen people. The message contained in the law and the prophets, as well as their experiences as a people in living that law and adhering to what the prophets revealed to them as found in the Old Testament. The law, as anchored in the Ten Commandments revealed to Moses; the covenants from the first given to Adam to the last given to David, by which His continued presence and commitment are revealed; and the experiences His chosen people went through in getting to, living in, and returning to the promised land.

Then, we go on through His words and actions, to reveal to us how and why He fulfilled that which His Father revealed as proclaimed in the New Testament. Telling us through the writings of the apostles and the Gospel accounts just how He fulfilled the Law, and by doing so, gave us the new and eternal covenant. And so, we are challenged to look at where we are in terms of our disposition to hear Him, to prepare ourselves to open our hearts and minds to enter into what the Church refers to as the Liturgy of the Word. For it is here where the message lays down the foundation by which we, as disciples, are enabled to experience the meaning of that message. But like any other experience, the disposition we bring to that experience will either enable us to understand His revelation clearly or cloud our ability to do so. This is a point well made by Belmonte[63] when he states that in hearing the word spoken to us, "We are faced with the reality of *choosing* (emphasis added) how we respond." He goes to challenge us who are exposed to the word to ask ourselves, Do we allow ourselves to "be captivated and transformed by it, or [do] we resist its action, thus despising the hand of God?" Put differently, we have to ask ourselves, How is it that we go about recognizing in the

---

[63] Belmonte, Charles. *Understanding the Mass.* Scepter Publications, Princeton, New Jersey, 1997, p. 79.

reading of the Scriptures and the proclaiming of the Gospel that it is the Word Himself speaking to us personally, pointedly, and profoundly?

Another personal example can again help me better illustrate what I mean. While teaching at a diocesan high school, I had the great joy of interacting with the various sports teams, one of which was the baseball team. Leaving school at the end of the day (during baseball season), I would get in my car, which was parked near the baseball field, to head home. I would notice the sounds made by the players and coaches at practice. But I would give them scant, if any, personal notice, other than recognize the baseball events as merely taking place. In short, I was merely a passerby with little or no personal involvement in the event taking place, as were those who were passing by the hill from which the Word spoke from His cross. When I would stop by to watch practice and sit in the stands, I would recognize the sounds for what they were: instruction, correction, encouragement, and so forth. In other words, I was, as a mere spectator, looking at the events on the field by which I was getting a better understanding of what was taking place through the words and interactions of the coaches and players. I was like those there standing down at the foot of Calvary while focusing on what the Word was saying, though not placing themselves in a position where others would recognize a commitment to the Word on their part. But on game days, when I was privileged to sit in the dugout with the players and coaches, I experienced on a personal and more intimate level not only of the sounds, but the actions and emotions associated with those sounds up close and personal. In short, I was involved in not only what was being said, but how the words spoken enabled the players and coaches to participate in the game in a fruitful and productive manner. It is as if I was among those standing alongside Mary and John at the foot of the cross and experiencing the Word up close and personal.

And it is in this challenge that we are asked to see where it is we find ourselves in listening to the Word. Are we among the passersby, finding ourselves on rocky ground? If so, will we make the effort to stop along whatever path we find ourselves and turn to the Word to not only listen, but hear what He is saying to us? Or are we finding ourselves in the "stands" among those spectators who hear the Word and find ourselves among the weeds? Will we make the effort to "sit up" and get engaged in a way that will enable us to better understand what is being said on "the field" (i.e., from the ambo)? Or are we among those who are in "the dugout" and find ourselves alongside those at the foot of the cross, standing on the good soil, focused on how we are interacting with the Word in a way that will enable us to see that we, by being personally immersed in His Word, are a part of the Word's team or beloved family? Why the challenge? Because the fruits of our efforts to hear the Word who speaks to us through the Scriptures will be intimately tied to the devotion by which we make the effort to hear Him.[64]

Now, it is time to look at just how Our Lord speaks to us through the Scriptures at the Holy Sacrifice of the Mass. First, we can look in terms of Scriptures to be read or proclaimed during the Liturgy of the Word. Then, we can understand why they are presented in the form and sequence we find them in the Mass. Finally, we can see how it is we, as disciples, are challenged to interact with these Scriptures, before, during, and after we have participated in the Mass.

THE FIRST READING

We start our journey through the Liturgy of the Word by going back to the Old Testament. Now, why do we start with the Old Testament? Because like the chosen people whose Scriptures they were, if nothing else, they are *anticipatory* in their approach to hearing what God had to reveal to them in those Scriptures. The Old Testament is, as Father Rich Keeszty points out, "a course of divine education preparing us for Jesus and promising us salvation in Him, which the New Testament attests the fulfillment of those promises."[65] Jesus declared this to be so, as first recorded in Luke, when as a teenager, He proclaimed to all who were present, that the message was fulfilled that day in Him.[66]

---

[64] Cf EP I. A subject that will be covered more clearly in the chapter on the Liturgy of the Eucharist.

[65] Father Rich Keeszty, Article in the Texas Catholic, April 24, 2014.

[66] Luke 4:21.

In short, because of the inseparable link between the Old and New Covenants, in celebrating the liturgy, the early Christians began with what was celebrated by those who attended the Synagogue and started with the Scriptures they possessed.[67] And as noted previously, we find them as a people, as a congregation, anticipatory. Whether it was regarding their entering into the promised land; the establishment of the Davidic Kingdom; the return from exile; or, most deliberately, most consistently, with increasing fervor, the coming of the awaited and promised messiah. They poured over the Torah to better understand the meaning and consequences associated the covenant God made with Moses. They pondered over the writings of the prophets as they reconciled the blessings and woes that would result from their being faithful or not to the covenant God made with David. And they would search through the history of their behavior in heeding God's word from the time of the covenant God made with Abraham through the events that led to their exile and the warnings of what awaited them in what they would experience upon their return.

However, in each and every case, the one constant we find in their relation to the Scriptures is their anticipation. Anticipating what it was that God Himself—and through His prophets—was commanding His people to do. And it was for this reason Jesus, as He tells us from the beginning of His public ministry, came to fulfill that law, not only by explaining its meaning, but more importantly, by showing them through His public ministry why they must do so. That is why we begin the Liturgy of the Word with the Old Testament.[68] That is why the Catechism of the Catholic Church (hereafter CCC) states the Old Testament "was deliberately so oriented that *it should prepare for and declare in prophecy the coming of Christ, redeemer of all men*" (emphasis added). Even though they contain matters imperfect and provisional, the books of the Old

---

[67] But that is where the similarity ends since the Jews found in their Synagogue worship that the Scriptures were sufficient in and of themselves; thus, their Liturgy did not end with a sacrifice, as from the beginning the Christian Liturgy did, as commanded by Our Lord.

[68] With the exception of the Easter season when the first reading is taken from the Acts of the Apostles.

Testament bear witness to the whole divine pedagogy of God's saving love: these writings "are a storehouse of sublime teaching on God and of sound wisdom on human life, as well as a wonderful treasury of prayers; in them, too, the mystery of our salvation is present in a hidden way."[69]

Not yet, however. For us to take the next step, we first have to be challenged through the message of anticipation spoken to us by the Father in the words, prophesies, and experiences revealed to us through the Old Testament. That step is for us to respond! To respond to the message of salvation that will be unveiled to us through the Psalms. A means by which we will prepare more deeply for our meeting with the messiah, who will first come to us in His Word and then in His real presence in the Eucharist. The Psalms, which we must not lose sight of, must be recognized as being antiphonal in nature. In the Psalms we find that it is not only God who talks to us, but the means by which we talk to God.

THE RESPONSORIAL PSALM

The Psalms, engage the entire story of salvation,[70] which the Catechism points out challenges us "to change our attitudes of prayer."[71] The Psalms are through which, if we truly listen, we will hear God speaking to us. It is almost, one might say,[72] that the Psalmist knows where we are in our disposition and that what we bring to the events we will experience by sharing His hour with Him. Yet depending on our disposition (whether it be that of the passerby, from afar, or being intimately up close to Him), we will find God, in speaking to us through the Psalmist, is talking to us in words appropriate to the circumstances in which we find ourselves. He does this with the specific intent of encouraging us to become more personally involved in the one, perfect, and unrepeatable sacrifice about to be re-presented in and through His Son. Yet as Athanasius points

---

[69] Catechism of the Catholic Church, Article 122.

[70] Bergsma, John. *Sacrifice of Praise, an Introduction to the Psalms.* Catholic Productions.

[71] CCC Art 2597.

[72] The approach I have taken here is in large part influenced by the 10 CD series by John Bergsma's *Sacrifice of Praise, an Introduction to the Psalms.*

out,[73] the Psalms, being unique from all other Scripture, give us the means for participating in worship by speaking for us, as they did for the Israelites passing through the Red Sea.

And thus, by their very nature, the Psalms are demanding of us our personal, interactive, and participative response to their message and their challenge, whether it be in deed or word. Yet as Brieg points out, it is a participation that can take on many forms, depending on the disposition we bring to our understanding of the Mass. Particularly, we can recognize this is a means by which we are given the opportunity to enter into a close and personal relationship with God. And if we are to take advantage of that opportunity, we must accept the fact that the Psalms require from us a response. A response that, if we truly listen, must be personal, because the God who is speaking to us through the Psalms is speaking to us personally. But here is where the challenge rears its head: the relationship which God wants with us—and for which He challenges us through the Palms—if it is to be genuine, requires that we speak to God as well. Thus, the object of the praying the Psalms during the liturgy (which can trace its origins to the earliest Jewish liturgies held in the Synagogues) is for us to enter into a dynamic and personal communion with the One whose hour we are asked by Him to spend with Him. And because of that challenge, we must recognize that the Psalms are not to be looked at, nor treated, as a performance—as magnificent the particular choir or soloist may be. No! The Psalms are to be treated for what they are: a personal dialogue between God and those of us who participate in the hour. By doing so, this becomes an outward and proactive demonstration of our disposition toward the One who is asking us to respond. A challenge that asks us to look at ourselves and see if we are not only are willing, but dare to, respond.

Another experience from my days at the diocesan high school can again better explain the point. It was from my experiences in teaching the students—here in terms of their responses to the questions I posed to them in class compared with their responses on Friday nights at home football games—that I use to make my point about the challenge for

---

[73] Athanasius. Praying the Psalms. https://www.prayerfoundation.org/

us in looking at how we respond to the one leading the Psalm offered in the Mass. In class, the response I would get from the students to my questions or challenges ranged from the indifferent to the enthusiastic. These responses, were directly related (as I learned after some thirteen years) to their interest in the subject, as well as their preparation for the class. The more interested they were in the subject or the more prepared they were to address the subject, the more enthusiastic their answers. Yet when I would meet them at the pep rally held before the football game, these same students responded to the events about to take place on the field with almost unanimous and genuine enthusiasm. They were giving their all to making sure the team knew they would not only be there, but that they were personally rooting for them. This is an attitude I propose the Psalmist is asking from those of us, whether priest celebrant, deacon assistant, Psalm leader, or parishioner: to see in our response to the Psalm offered an indication of our anticipation of the events that will soon take place during the Liturgy of the Eucharist.

In other words, the Psalms, to which we are asked to respond, put us in the shoes of those high school students. And in doing so, they challenge us, in terms of our responses, to ask ourselves if our response is one we are compelled to make (as is the response asked for by the teacher in the classroom) or one we desire to make (as is the response offered in cheering for the team that is about to take the field). In other words, in terms of our anticipation of the messiah, are we responding as we would in class, in dread of the grade that awaits our answer, or as we would at the pep rally, in excited anticipation of the victory that we will share in—or, put differently, as an experience?

For it is the Psalms that prepare us for, by whetting our sense of anticipation, the events that will surround the arrival of the messiah. And now, we will be more clearly exposed to this by our entering into what the Word has prepared for us through the readings of the New Testament. First, from the epistles written by the apostles and, then, through the words proclaimed by the Evangelists in the Gospel.

The challenge for us, who find ourselves about to begin our journey into the New Testament (whether as passersby, distant observers, or close to the One who is speaking to us), is to ask ourselves the following: Is our anticipation, our desire, and our commitment to what we will now hear from Him, through the writings of the apostles and Evangelists, where it should be? Will we truly hear what He has to say to us to prepare us to meet Him in a sacramental and most perfect way, which we will do by communing with Him in His body, blood, soul and divinity in the Liturgy of the Eucharist? The answer will be directly influenced by the approach we have taken to the Old Testament message given to us in the first reading, which will set, for the most part, the approach we will find ourselves in now.

THE SECOND READING

We are here. We have arrived. In whichever way our disposition has been leading us, we are now exposed to the reality of the Messiah, in the person of Jesus being present. But as in any relationship, we find in our participation in the Mass that our relationship with Jesus is evolving. We will now be exposed to Him from the experiences of His apostles and His early followers who founded the first Christian communities. Thus, as disciples, we are called to hear what the apostles shared of their personal experiences with Him in terms of what He has said and did with them. And this they did by explaining how those experiences would set the baseline for how those who choose to follow Him were expected to live their lives as disciples. That through their encounter with the Risen Lord, they are sharing their commitment to living the message Our Lord left with them to also share with the whole world, giving us a continuing example for living our particular call to discipleship. That what He asked of them, He is asking of those of us now, who have responded to His call through our baptism. Because the words we hear spoken by the apostles through their epistles, whether written to specific communities and individuals (as does Paul and the author of the Letter to the Hebrews) or to the Church universal (as does Peter, John, James, and Jude), are not historical. No, they are "living words" that are as "relevant today as when they were first enunciated."[74] And it is in our receptivity

---

[74] Oury, p. 62.

to what those apostles chose to share with us in their writings that will influence our not only our receptivity of Him but, more importantly, to the world in which we are called to live as His disciples. But again, this requires that we place ourselves in the Scriptures being read to us. That we truly become a part of the community then as we are a part of the community now hearing the Word of God spoken to us.

For the word to transform us from wherever we find ourselves to where He desires us to be, we must not merely passively listen to, but personally accept, the message He has for us in the words given to us by His apostles. Let me give you a personal experience that may help me better explain what I mean. During my deacon formation program many years ago, we took a class on Pauline theology. The professor was a Jesuit priest with many years of teaching Pauline theology at Georgetown University. In answering the several quizzes given to us on the Pauline letters, I *knew* well enough the content and message of Paul's letters to earn an A for the course. At the conclusion of the course, the professor called me over and said, "Nick, in reading your exam answers and your paper, I am interested in knowing why you are so angry with Paul?" Wow! Was I? And if so, how did he pick up on that? I thought about it and said, "Father, I think you can say that I am a 'Peter fan,' and I guess you can say I am angry that Peter doesn't get the same recognition that Paul does." He was appreciative that I would share that with him and then said, "I want you to spend some time reflecting on this. Think of how powerful Jesus was to take His most powerful enemy and turn him into His most powerful advocate." Well, after that challenge, I came to realize that although I *knew* what was in Paul's letters, I didn't really **know** what it was that Paul was telling me. After that experience, I went back and found, for example, how I was to live as a disciple in Romans; how I was to deal with trials and temptations in 1 and 2 Corinthians; and, more importantly, for me who then was preparing to be His servant in the Order of Deacon, what Our Lord was asking of me in 1 Timothy and Philippians. In short, although for the longest time I was listening to what Paul was saying in his epistles, I really wasn't hearing him; thus, I was not allowing him to help me live my diaconia in the way Our Lord was asking of me to serve Him. Hence, if one can truly say that they had not merely listened passively to what was being read through the letters of the apostles but instead personally heard what the letters were saying to them at that moment, they would "no longer be the same person they were before."[75] They would become, for example, like John and the Magdalene, proclaiming the good news of the Risen Lord to all those they came into contact with rather than like the authorities and passersby who went on their way still looking for the One who has already come.

THE GOSPEL

We come now to the point where we are presented with the Word Himself. No longer are we limited to listening to those whom His Father empowered to reveal His coming through the writings of the Old Testament. No longer are we asked to listen to the accounts of those whom His Son commanded teach us about their personal experiences with His works and His words, as revealed in their New Testament writings. No! We are now invited to meet with Him in person. We are now given the opportunity to hear the Word Himself proclaim to us the good news. And by doing so, we can hear what it is that He expects of us, who dare claim to be His disciples.

We are now challenged to listen to Him first hand, telling us what He meant by coming to do His Father's will, by fulfilling His Father's law. Which He does through His proclamation of the good news, the Gospel through the ordained minister who does so acting *in persona christi*.[76] Thus, as the "*ipissima verba*," the very words of Christ, "must stand apart from, and therefore set off from the other readings." For "it is by faith that we know that Christ, present in His own words [is Himself] proclaiming the Gospel."[77]

---

[75] Belmonte, p. 79.

[76] Recognizing, that if it be the deacon doing so, then it is *in persona Christi servitus*, whereas if there is no deacon present and it is the priest doing so, he is acting *in persona Christi capitus*.

[77] GIRM No. 9.

Thus, when the Gospel is proclaimed, it is not merely a reflection or even a remembrance, but a personal and intimate experience with the Word made flesh.[78] And yet as it is with any experience, it is the disposition we bring to the experience that will either make clear or cloud what it is we take away from that experience, here in terms of the effect it will have on us.[79] Or as a priest described it quoting Bishop Fulton Sheen, will it be with apathy, antiphony, or sympathy?[80] On a personal note, as I reflect on this reality, I go back to my ordination day, when the bishop, placing a Book of the Gospels in my hand, reminds me in no uncertain terms that as I receive the book, I must never lose sight of the fact that I am a "herald of the Gospel." And as such, I "must believe what I read; teach what I believe; [and, where the 'rubber meets the road'] live what I teach." The same challenge, though not with the same sacramental commitment one enters into through their ordination, to all who hear the Gospel. That those who hear His Gospel message, must also look at their particular call to discipleship, whether that discipleship is lived as clergy, religious, or lay person, and ask themselves the following: Do we believe what we just heard proclaimed? Do we have the courage to share, through our discipleship, what it is we heard proclaimed with others? And as it is for me, both sacramentally and personally, do we have the confidence in the Word just proclaimed to live what we heard and do so in a way that makes His presence and His love manifest to those we encounter through our personal call to discipleship?

One way for me that makes it easy to remember His challenge is to think about what it is we are doing. When preparing to hearing Him speak to us in the Gospel, we silently cross ourselves on our forehead, on our lips, and on our heart. This is a gesture that is explained so beautifully by Alyson Rockhold in an article she wrote for the website <u>Busted Halo</u>: "We cross our forehead so that the Word of God may be in our thoughts and purify our minds. We cross our lips so that our speech may be holy and incline us to share the Gospel with others. And we cross our hearts

---

[78] This subject is covered in depth by Father Oury, *The Mass*, pp. 58-60.

[79] As explained so clearly by Our Lord in His parable of the Sower as found in Matthew 13:1-23.

[80] Personal conversation with a priest in the sacristy after mass on February 23, 2022.

to invite God to strengthen our love for him and others. All of this is so that we might know, proclaim, and love Jesus Christ all the more."[81]

But before He begins to speak, as He approaches us and as He prepares to speak with us, we are asked, as were the many in the crowds that came to hear Him speak during His public ministry, to recognize Him, to greet His presence among us as we would do for any dignitary for who He is. Whether it be, for example, the bishop coming into the parish schoolhouse or the president coming to a function. In preparing for His arrival in the Gospel, we are asked to make some overt, public act that shows we recognize his arrival. And that we do, in our welcoming Him to speak to us through the Gospel by our Alleluia acclamation.

This is an acclamation that we find the GIRM identifying as a "credal statement of faith in Jesus" and, as such, is "a rite or act in itself by which the gathering of the faithful welcomes and greets the Lord who is about to speak."[82] This is the same acclamation that Oury describes as "being sung by celestial choirs in the Book of Revelation, which describes the Liturgy of Eternity."[83] The Alleluia, "one of the two Hebrew words that have endured, untranslated, for use in the Mass (the other is Amen)."[84] The Alleluia, which is a Latin translation of "HALELU YAH," which in Hebrew means "Praise God."[85] Thus, the Alleluia is an acclamation by which we are challenged to reveal the enormity of our recognition of Him. A word that is meant "to be heard by attentive ears and received

---

[81] She goes on in her article to give us some historical background about the gesture. She points out that the <u>first record of making the sign of the cross before the Gospel proclamation was in the ninth century.</u> Benedictine Monk Remigius of Auxerre (d. c. 908) wrote that the congregation signed their foreheads as the deacon signed his forehead and breast.

Later, this practice was solidified by Pope Innocent in the eleventh century. He declared that the deacon would make the sign of the cross on the Bible, and then together with the congregation, everyone would sign their foreheads, lips, and chests. Alyson Rockhold, "Head, Lips and Heart: Learning About Unity Through the Three Cross Prayer." *Busted Halo*, April 30, 2021.

[82] GIRM No 63.

[83] Oury p. 68.

[84] Wuerl, Donald Cardinal. *The Mass.* Doubleday, New York, 2011, p. 14.

[85] Oury p. 68.

by eager hearts."[86] An acclamation we find will by our response, to vary, depending again on our disposition.

The challenge is to ask, Where do we find ourselves in our acclaiming Him? Do we find ourselves doing so in a perfunctory manner, as did the passersby that First Friday? Or do we find ourselves acclaiming Him by a distant and somewhat conditional recognition of His Presence, as did those that day from afar? Or do we, as did Mary, the Magdalene, and John—who we can envision representing the innocent, the penitent, and the priesthood, and who each, according to their relationship with Him—acclaim His presence with the same public and intimate intensity that they not only displayed at the foot of the cross, but in their words and deeds upon leaving that hill? A disposition that will establish for us the degree of receptivity by which we will find ourselves not only approaching, but accepting the message He is proclaiming, which, in turn, will determine how open we will be to the exposition of that message in the homily.

THE HOMILY

Our Lord has just proclaimed to us by sharing with us through His words and examples what it is He is asking of those who wish to follow Him as disciples. Yet He doesn't stop there. He desires that what He has revealed to us through the Gospel be made relevant to the particular time, place, and circumstances we find ourselves living our particular discipleship. And this He does through the voice of His ordained minister in what is known as the ***homily***. The homily, which Pope Francis points out in his Apostolic Exhortation *Evangelii Gaudium,* has "special importance because of its eucharistic context: it surpasses all forms of catechesis as the supreme moment in the dialogue between God and his people which lead up to sacramental communion. *The homily takes up once more the dialogue which the Lord has already established with his people*" (emphasis

---

[86] Guardini, Romano. *Meditations before Mass.* Sophia Institute Press, Manchester, New Hampshire, 1955, p. 71.

added).[87] This is why the Catechism states that the "Liturgical Homily takes pride of place among all forms of Christian instruction."[88] It is true that for some (I pray not many) the homily can be experienced as a challenge—because not all homilists are, or could even be, for example, another Bishop Barron or Bishop Sheen. Yet as Hahn so adroitly points out, "Just as Jesus comes to us in humble, tasteless wafers, so the Holy Spirit sometimes works through a monotone, lackluster preacher."[89] For me, personally, that strikes home because I find myself frequently going back to Saint Paul's admonition to those called to serve God in his first letter to the Corinthians. For in it, he warns us that God chooses the "foolish," the "weak," the "lowly," and the "despised" to do His work for us so that we may know that any good that comes from our preaching is to be recognized as belonging to God and not us.[90]

And that work, in terms of the homily, is to "guide the assembly, [as well as] the preacher, to a life-changing communion with Christ in the Eucharist. This means that the words of the preacher must be measured, so that the Lord, more than his minister, will be the center of attention."[91] In short, the one given the responsibility to act in the person of Christ in making relevant to today the message Our Lord proclaimed in the Gospel must never lose sight of the reality that he is not called on to give a performance on but rather an exhortation of the message Our Lord intends those spending an hour with Him to receive.

Yet what we preach, as I have learned from the feedback I receive (as I suspect is the case with many other priests and deacons), is not necessarily what is heard. In short, as the Lord learned; as I have learned; and what others have learned is that true communication does not occur until the

---

87 Pope Francis Evangelii Gaudium (The joy of the Gospel). Article 137. It Is important to note that the Holy Father thinks so seriously on this aspect of the liturgy that he devotes *17* articles to this particular subject (Articles 135–151).
88 CCC Article 132.
89 Hahn, Scott. *The Lamb's Supper: The Mass as Heaven and Earth.* Doubleday, 1999, p. 48.
90 1 Corinthians 1:26-31.
91 Evangelii Gaudium, No. 138.

receiver receives. That what one may believe to be a "great" homily in terms of the preparation for, the content of, and delivery of the message may turn out to be (in human terms) a "bust." But I have also learned that homilies I prepared "in haste" and delivered somewhat disjointedly turned out to be well received. Both experiences, at least for me, are confirmation that it is not the homilist, but the One in whose voice He speaks with that is the determiner of what the message He desires be sent. On the other hand, the effectiveness of what is communicated, in terms of what is heard is, in turn, determined by the disposition one brings to their openness to that message. For those who walk in the shoes of the "passersby" may hear merely words that are of minimal impact on their particular journey. Those, on the other hand, who find themselves standing in the company of the ones found at the base of the hill may recognize Who is speaking but not realize that it is to them that His message is intended. Those who find themselves standing at the foot of the cross may find that they, like Mary, John, and the Magdalene, experience not only the personal impact of the homilist's words, but also the encouragement that this message has in deepening their commitment to do His will. Because the Word, as Guardini describes it, has one purpose: "It is meant to be heard by attentive ears and received by eager hearts."[92]

Thus, the effectiveness of the homily can only be measured by how it "help[s] the Word make [the] transition to practical life." By encouraging us to "reformulate the problems in our lives that we want to reform."[93] In other words, as Belmonte points out, if we have truly heard what the Word is saying to us, "We can no longer be the same person we were before. Either we allow ourselves to be transformed by it, or we resent its actions, thus despising the hand of God."[94] When we stop and think about it, this is the same choice that the disciples on the road to

---

[92] Guardini, Romano. *Meditations before Mass.* Sophia Institute Press, Manchester, New Hampshire, 1955, p. 71.

[93] Oury, Guy, Rev. *The Mass.* Catholic Book Publishing Company, New York, 1988, pp. 65, 70.

[94] Belmonte, Charles. *Understanding the Mass.* Scepter Publications, Princeton, New Jersey, 1997, p. 79.

Emmaus were faced with. To choose to remain in their disappointment/discouragement at what they "heard" from Jerusalem or to choose to hear the Word Himself and, by doing so, find their hearts burning.[95]

We are now at the point in the Mass where God, who began His discourse with us through the inspired words of the priests, prophets, and kings of the Old Testament and His apostles in the New Testament has achieved what He wanted in the person of His Son, the Word, speaking personally to us through the Gospels and the homily. He now asks us, in a similar way He asked His apostles to profess who they believed Him to be, to stand and profess what it is we believe of Him, His Father, the Holy Spirit, and His Church. This is a belief that although being constant from the beginning has, through the inspiration of the Holy Spirit, become clearer over the many centuries from its first proclamation at the time of the apostles to the present day. This is a belief we profess in our reciting the Creed.

THE CREED

We have now heard from the writers of the Old Testament telling us from under the inspiration of the Holy Spirit what the Father, in summation, by His covenantal love promised us: the coming of the messiah. The coming of His Son, through the fiat of the virgin.[96] We next heard from the apostles, also inspired by the same Spirit, that the covenantal love of the Son for us, as manifested so perfectly in His sacrifice on the cross, would be sufficient for us to deal with any and all experiences our particular journey of discipleship may bring us.[97] That in persevering in our discipleship, we will also share in the joy of the resurrection.

But we also learned that His message did not stop there with the inspired words of the apostles. No. We find Jesus Himself in the words He speaks to us through the ordained minister proclaiming the Gospel *in persona christi*, telling us what He wants us to hear from Him first hand. He

---

[95] Luke 24:13-35.
[96] cf. Isaiah 7:14.
[97] cf. II Cor 12:9.

wants to personally tell us not only what it is He will ask of us who wish to be His disciples, but what He will do for us as His disciples. This is a message of encouragement, while at the same time, it is a message that carries with it a challenge. A message that calls for a response. And it is here that we find ourselves challenged to literally "stand up and be counted." To publicly profess what it is that we are committing to. What it is that we believe. What is it that we profess. It is the Creed. The Creed, which distills the basic outline of what it means to be a Christian into a short summation that belies the depth and richness of what it proclaims. The Creed, which the Church took almost four hundred years to articulate.[98] The Creed, which has stood the test of time, from the age of the apostles to the present, and will continue to do so until He comes again as the preeminent testament to Christian orthodoxy.

The Creed, by which we are challenged to profess in four ways what it is we believe. We profess first, that the Father, is the ***"maker of heaven and earth, of all things visible and invisible."*** And by doing so, we are saying "yes" to the truth that the Father so loved us that even before we were conceived in His image and likeness, He knew us. And that even before we were born, He had a plan as to how we would be a valuable fit in the workings of His kingdom.[99] The challenge for us, then, as we speak these words, gives us the opportunity to ask ourselves: Do we *truly* believe that He loves us that much? Then, we are challenged to profess our faith in His Son, Jesus Christ. Do we *truly* believe that He is ***"the Only Begotten Son of God, born of the Father before all ages. God from God, Light from Light, true God from true God, begotten, not made, consubstantial with the Father; through him all things were made. For us men and for our salvation he came down from heaven, and by the Holy Spirit was incarnate of the Virgin Mary, and became man. For our sake, he was crucified under Pontius Pilate. He suffered death and was buried, and rose again on the third day in accordance with the***

---

[98] Having first to deal with, at the Council of Ephesus (321 AD) ,the truth that Jesus is true God and true man and then at the Council of Constantinople (381 AD) the truth that the Holy Spirit is truly God.

[99] cf. Jerimiah 1

Scriptures. He ascended into heaven and is seated at the right hand of the Father. He will come again in glory to judge the living and the dead, and his kingdom will have no end?" This is a question posed to Peter and the apostles. A question that remained prevalent, as we saw, for almost four hundred years after He returned to His Father. A question that we find, sadly, being asked again in the secular world in which we find ourselves living our particular call to discipleship. A question, unfortunately, that will be asked and will have to be responded to by you, me, and all who are members of His body until He comes again. Next, we are challenged to profess our faith in the truth of the Holy Spirit being God by proclaiming that the Holy Spirit is *"the Lord, the giver of life, who proceeds from the Father and the Son, who with the Father and the Son is adored and glorified, who has spoken through the prophets."* The same Spirit that Jesus promised He would ask the Father to give us; to be with us always. He will be, Our Lord promises us, "the Spirit of truth." The Holy Spirit, who once coming into our lives, for the first time at our baptism, whose presence will be strengthened at our confirmation, and who will remain with us, and will be in us.[100] But again, the challenge is one the world is unwilling to face up to: God's love as manifested in the person of the Holy Spirit. A love so intense; so unconditional; and so powerful that those of the world look upon the Spirit's presence as they would by looking into a bright sun and turn away from that love. Or they choose to deal with that presence by wearing "spiritual sunglasses," by which the intensity of that love will be diminished. The challenge that finds us having to ask, Do we *truly* believe that love, as manifested in the person of the Holy Spirit, is not only with us but *in* us?

Finally, we come to our last challenge in professing our faith through our recitation of the Creed: the challenge to publicly profess our belief in His *"one, holy, catholic, and apostolic Church."* To believe all that it teaches in terms of faith and morals. To believe all the truths revealed to us completely and with finality up to the death of the last apostle. For example, the truths that begin with God's purpose for conception; His

---

[100] cf. John 14:16-17

intention as to how our earthly life must end; the covenantal meaning and purpose for the creation of man to be who he is meant to be and woman to be who she was created to be. To the reality of the efficacious effects of the seven Sacraments, as instituted by Christ Himself.[101] The truth of the apostolic succession as evidenced in the lineage of the Holy Father, as well as of those bishops who are in union with the Holy Father. The reality that our sins are forgiven through the absolution of the priest, who, in the Sacrament of Reconciliation, does so *in persona christi.* And ultimately, as we prepare to enter into the experience of the Liturgy of the Eucharist, to profess our belief in the reality of the truth that Jesus Christ, Himself will—though the words of consecration spoken by the priest *in persona christi*—become really present under the appearances of bread and wine in His glorified body, blood, soul and divinity.[102] A reality denied by non-Christians and, sadly, by some Catholics as well. Therefore, as we state our belief in His Church, we need to ask ourselves: Do we truly believe in all that it teaches?

For it is in and through the Church; the Church that is entrusted through its magisterium to hold fast and guard these truths; His Church through which He makes His presence known to the world where both His disciples and non-disciples live that He interacts with that world. And thus, He asks His Church, His body, and His disciples to pray for not only His disciples but for those who are non-disciples as well. To ask not only on our behalf, but theirs as well, that they come to not only recognize but experience His presence; His love; His encouragement; and His promises in their lives. And this we do through the Universal Prayer of the Church.

---

[101] Albeit, other than the Sacrament of Baptism and the Sacrament of the Eucharist, Our Lord has left it up to His Apostles and their successors as to the ritual by which the other Sacraments may be confected.

[102] A subject that will be addressed more thoroughly below, in the chapter on the Liturgy of the Eucharist.

THE UNIVERSAL PRAYER

The Universal Prayer of the Church, or the general intercessions or the Prayers of the Faithful,[103] have been a part of the Church's liturgical worship since the early church.[104] Yet since the sixth century, we find these prayers disappearing from the Roman Liturgy.[105] It was not until the VCII some 1400 years later that the fathers of the council called for the "restoration of the Universal Prayer in the reform of the Sacred Liturgy." The fathers went on to state that it was to be restored "after the Gospel and the homily."[106]

Thus, it was the intent of the fathers that after being exposed to the promises, experiences, and the good news as made relevant to those present through the homily, who, as disciples, are now called to respond "in some sense to the Word of God [just] received in faith, by exercising [*their*] *baptismal Priesthood*" (emphasis added).[107] And therein lies the challenge for us who are present at the Mass. We must ask ourselves, "How willing are we to *exercise* our 'baptismal priesthood?'"

How willing are we to recognize that we, as a member of the One, Holy, Catholic, and Apostolic Church, are related in some way to all who are—whether directly through their baptism or indirectly through their being His image and likeness—and, thus, are members of that same body? How willing are we to commit to be there for them in their needs, their trials, and their challenges? Whether this be the Holy Father,

---

[103] GIRM No 9. Of note is the reason for these prayers being identified as the Prayers of the Faithful. For in the Mass prior to VCII, the two parts were the Mass of the Catechumenate and the Mass of the Faithful. The catechumenate were excused after the homily, and it was the faithful who remained and who offered up these prayers. It is interesting to note that in the dismissal of RCIA candidates and catechumenates at mass, they are still today dismissed after the homily.

[104] In fact, it is the oldest Christian prayer not contained in Sacred Scripture. Oury, Guy, Rev. *The Mass.* Catholic Book Publishing Company, New York, 1988, p. 96.

[105] But they always remained a part of the Good Friday liturgy.

[106] Sacrosanctum Concilium No. 53.

[107] GIRM No. 69.

whose focus is on the salvation of souls, or the individual whose focus is on the destruction of that church? In other words, will our faith be strong enough to recognize that we are not alone? That we are not only sons and daughters of the Father, but also brothers and sisters with all who were created by Him through the same love by which He create us? In other words, we are challenged through these prayers to ask ourselves, "What is truly our disposition to not only our praying for our needs, but for the needs of others as well?" This is a challenge that encompasses the needs of the Church; public authorities; the salvation of the whole world; those burdened by any kind of difficulty; and those of the local community (whether they be its communal needs or the needs of its individual members).[108]

Of interest to note is that it falls to the deacon to announce these prayers.[109] Why is that? Because the intentions—as in most instances as read today—are often drafted from a "global" or "prepared" source, while originally, they came from the community itself.[110] It was one of these intentions for which the fathers of the council restored the Order of Deacon to its proper place in the Church's hierarchy. They were to live among what Pope Francis refers to as the "sheep." That in doing so, they would be better able to "smell the sheep." They would be better able to discern their needs, thus being the one better suited to bring those needs to the attention of the Church.[111] This is why, as it was in the early church and is once again now, the deacon's role to bring those needs before the congregation during the Mass through the General Intercessions. Because as Irwin points out, it "was [the deacon] who knew the particular needs of the community." Thus, because of that, it "reflects his ministry outside the Mass."[112]

---

[108] Ibid. No. 70.

[109] Ibid No. 71.

[110] Which is still the case, particularly in the intentions offered for specific members of the community who have died, and it is a member of the family who brings that particular intention to the notice of the parish community.

[111] A subject covered in more depth in my book *Who Do You Say That I Am? A Deacon's Perspective of the Diaconate.* Amazon Press, 2021.

[112] Irwin, Kevin W. *Response to 101 Questions on the Mass.* Paulist Press, New York/ Mahwah, New Jersey, 1999, p. 69.

Thus, the prayers offered in the Universal Prayer are looked on by the council fathers as the "cap[ping of] the Liturgy of the Word in a way similar to the reception of Holy Communion at the end of the Liturgy of the Eucharist."[113] They are a means by which the baptized commit themselves to pray "for the holy Church, for civil authorities, for those weighed down by various needs, for all men and women, and for the salvation of the whole world."[114] Taking it a step further, what one can see is that these prayers present us, whether the one announcing them or the ones responding to them, with the challenge to have the disposition, once the Mass has ended, to implement what they are praying for in the way they live their particular call to discipleship.

With the conclusion of these prayers, we become aware of the reality that we have concluded the Liturgy of the Word and find ourselves leaving the "Table of the Word," from which we have been "nourished with the doctrine of the Lord." Now, we need to make the effort to ask ourselves the following: "How is it we have prepared ourselves to approach the 'Table of the Eucharist,' from which we will receive 'our food, the "Bread of Life?"'[115] Passively (as did the passersby to the events about to occur on the hill of Calvary)? With trepidation (as did those who were watching passively from the foot of the hill)? Or with a personal commitment to not only gain from, but share, in some intimate way (as was the case with Mary, John, and the Magdalene) in the sacrifice for which He came and for which His hour was meant?

---

[113] Sacrosanctum Concilium No. 53.
[114] GIRM No. 69.
[115] Oury, p. 70.

CHAPTER THREE: THE LITURGY OF THE EUCHARIST

THE OFFERTORY

The time has arrived. The event for which our participation in the Liturgy of the Word has prepared us for is about to take place. And like any other event, there needs to be a period of preparation. The impending sacrifice that is to take place on the hill of Calvary, to which Our Lord has willing consented to, is no different. Then, it was the Roman soldiers and those enlisted to support them by their preparation activities who enabled the sacrifice to take place. Activities in which they gathered the vertical beam on which the horizontal crossbar to which Jesus would be nailed to the cross would be fixed.[116] For example, they would need the nails that would enable them to attach his hands and feet to the cross. The vinegary wine that would be offered to dull the pain of the crucifixion. The hyssop branch by which to offer that wine. And the hammer and spear by which to ensure the crucified were really dead. Now, in the Mass, it is the deacon and the acolytes, who through their preparation activities, which begin with the accepting of the bread and wine from members of the congregation that will be used by the priest to offer that same sacrifice re-presented (albeit in an unbloody manner) to take place. There is preparing of the paten on which the bread will be laid; the chalice in which the wine will be placed is prepared by the deacon. I find great significance on a personal (maybe sacramental) level the words I speak over the chalice in preparing it for the priest to offer in sacrifice, the words that tell us what Jesus, through His incarnation did, and we, through our faith, aspire to. What it is we who are there ought to strive for in terms of taking away from this sacrifice to live our personal

---

[116] Since the actual form of the cross is not specified in the Gospels, there are those who believe it to be what is referred to as the *crux immissa* (which is a familiar shape of the cross found in Roman Catholic churches) and those who refer to it as the *crux commissa* (which is the shape of the familiar Franciscan "tau" cross). In either case, all agree that Jesus was crucified and died on the cross on Calvary.

call to discipleship? For in pouring the wine and then the water into the chalice, I silently say the following prayer, "By the mystery of this wine and water, may we come to share in the divinity of Christ, who humbled Himself to share in our humanity."[117]

This is a prayer that presents us with both a statement of certitude, in terms of our faith in Jesus who became man, as well as a challenge of discipleship. In terms of our faith, it affirms that through Mary's *fiat*, the Son of God became man in his humanity. That in His humanity, He experienced all that we experience in life: hunger (Mark 11:12, as He was leaving Bethany with His disciples); thirst (John 4:7, in His encounter with the Samaritan woman at the well); loneliness (John 1:10-11, when the people whom He lived among didn't recognize Him); anger (John 2:12-16, as He cleansed the temple); fear (Luke 22:41-44, in the Garden of Gethsemane); rejection (Matt 8:34, by the Gadarenes); denial (Mark 14:29-31, by Peter in the courtyard of the high priest); betrayal (Luke 22:4-6, by Judas to the religious authorities); and even death (John 19:30, from His cross).

In terms of its challenge, it is asking us to recognize that by sharing in Jesus' divinity, we must do three things. First, we are challenged to commit to His commandment to love as He loves us, which when you get right down to it, is nothing less that *unconditional love*. Then, it challenges us to recognize that as disciples we, too, like the forgiving Father, must make His unquenchable mercy visible to all we encounter through our discipleship. And finally, it challenges us to offer unconditional forgiveness to all our discipleship brings us in contact with.

---

[117] A subject addressed in great detail by Deacon William T. Ditewig in his article "The Mixture of Water and Wine" in *The Deacon*, where he states, "The practice of adding water to the wine used for the sacrifice goes back almost to the beginning, and there has always been a strong symbolic meaning given it. The water represents all of humanity, human nature itself, while the wine represents Christ." He then goes on to quote Cyprian, who said, "The key issue here was not the commingling in itself but what it expressed." Then he goes on to challenge his brother deacons to reflect on our inner dispositions as we do these things. Do we handle the vessels with care? Do we act with some solemnity in our movements? Do we truly internalize the words we are privileged to pray as we add the water to the wine?" This is a challenge I believe all who are participating in the holy sacrifice of the Mass ought to do.

Tying this all together is the corporal on which the bread and wine, which will be transformed by the words of consecration later to be said by the priest, acting *in persona christi* into the body, blood, soul and divinity of Christ, is placed. [118] The stage is now set. The preparations are made. The event is now ready to take place through the Eucharistic Prayer.

THE EUCHARISTIC PRAYER

It begins! The sacrifice of Calvary is to be re-presented. The new Adam, who came to atone for the sin of the first Adam, is to do so by offering Himself in sacrifice. The Lamb of God who came to take away the sins of the world is now willingly, obediently, and lovingly giving His life to His Father as satisfaction for our sins. This is a reality that will be made manifest through the prayer of the Church known as the Eucharistic Prayer.[119] This is a prayer in which the bread and wine offered becomes, through the words of consecration, the body, blood, soul, and divinity of the Christ whose sacrifice[120] it is. A sacrifice that we not only ask to be looked upon by the Father as He did upon Abel's sacrifice; as He did on Melchizedek's sacrifice; and as He did on Abraham's sacrifice[121], but to do so in a way that allows us to experience the reality that it is one accepted most favorably by the Father because it is being offered by His Son.

Thus, the Eucharistic Prayer is the means by which those of us who participate in the Mass, in whatever manner appropriate to our particular call to discipleship, are mysteriously transported to the hill of Calvary. It

---

[118] This subject will be addressed more fully when we address the Eucharistic Prayer.

[119] Which, since the sixth century, has been the same (with minor revisions) until Saint Paul VI in issuing his Missale Romanum in 1970 expanded the number; until today, we find there are the four commonly used Eucharistic Prayers (to be addressed), as well as others used for special purposes, such as for Masses of Reconciliation and for various needs. However, ***all have one purpose: to enable the sacrifice of Calvary to be made present through the words of consecration, which remain constant in each***.

[120] In his book *The Holy Sacrifice of the Mass*, McGuckian points out that **"if we do not understand sacrifice, we do not understand the Eucharist, and we do not understand the Church."**

[121] Belmonte, Charles. *Understanding the Mass.* Scepter Publications, Princeton, New Jersey, 1997, p. 149.

is a prayer by which those present mystically find themselves immersed in the "hours from the lifting up of Jesus' own heart to the Father to the moment of His death and resurrection. Those many hours [being] condensed to a few paragraphs."[122] A prayer that "carries us back"[123] to the events that began that Thursday night in the upper room and culminated with the empty tomb in the glory of the resurrection. A prayer so powerful that through it, we are given the opportunity to "bring to life" the events surrounding the perfect sacrifice offered that Friday on Calvary by the Son to His Father. A prayer by which we experience the renewal of the mysteries of the Life of Christ. A prayer by which we experience the renewal of the incarnation. A prayer by which we experience the renewal of Christ's passion. A prayer by which we experience the renewal of Christ's resurrection.[124] This is why the prayer begins with our proclaiming that it is "right and just" to give thanks to "the Lord our God" for what we are about to enter into and that is concludes with our affirmation that "all glory and honor" belongs to God, Father, Son, and Holy Spirit.

However, it is between its opening and closing that the mystery of Calvary, the sacrifice of Jesus, becomes present. Where the incarnate God offers Himself to His Father through the intercession of the Holy Spirit. It is an intimate and unconditional experience that those of us present are privileged to not merely witness, but truly participate in. And it is here that we are challenged. To ask ourselves how committed we are to truly open not only our hearts, but our lives to the reality of Christ's paschal mystery in which we are personally involved. How genuinely do we acclaim that the sacrifice unfolding is an **atoning sacrifice**, a sacrifice offered *for the forgiveness of sins*? How truly do we recognize that it is not only Our Lord's sacrifice

---

[122] King, William J., Msgr. "A Look At the Eucharistic Prayers." Simplycatholic.com, September 1, 2021.

[123] Which is why the Eucharistic Prayer is also known as the "*anaphora*," a word used in the Church's liturgy as early as the third century, which is the Greek word "to carry back."

[124] Muller, Michael, Fr. *The Holy Sacrifice of the Mass*. Tan Books, Rockford, Illinois, 1992, pp. 150–233.

being offered in the Mass, ***but ours as well?***[125] This is a challenge made evident in Eucharistic Prayer I, where it is acknowledged that the "faith and devotion" with which we participate in the sacrifice of the Mass is *"**known to [God]**."*[126]

Thus, we can say, along with Msgr. King, that the Eucharistic Prayer is "the center and core of the Mass."[127] It is the means by which the sacrifice is re-presented. It is the means by which we are enabled to experience the events surrounding Jesus' passion, death, resurrection, and ascension.

The Eucharistic Prayer, as previously noted,[128] remained constant in content since at least the third century, and, since formalized by the Council of Trent, had been the only form found in the Missal known then as the Canon—until other options were promulgated by Saint Pope Paul VI in 1970. What is interesting to note is that in looking at the four main Eucharistic Prayers, we can see the richness of the Church's history being unveiled in relation to the one constant: the making present of Jesus through the words of consecration in the Sacrament of the Eucharist. Also of note is that whichever of the prayers used, they all have the same components (which we will look at individually below).[129]

The efforts which began from the end of the council to add additional Eucharist Prayers culminated with the approval of Saint Pope Paul VI in 1968 to add three additional prayers to the traditional prayer, then known as the Roman Canon, and which now became known as Eucharistic Prayer I. The promulgation of the approval of the additional

---

[125] Eucharistic Prayer III.

[126] Which is why McGuckian poses the question, "{H}ow many people I our Eucharistic Congregation really intend to sacrifice?"

[127] King, William J., Msgr. "A Look at the Eucharistic Prayers." Simplycatholic.com, September 1, 2021.

[128] See Footnote 1 above.

[129] The following narration is based on the information contained in the Adoremus Bulletin article "From One Eucharistic Prayer to Many: How it Happened and Why?" Father Cassian Folsom, OSB Online Edition Vol II Nos. 4-6: September-November 1996.

prayers came with the issuance of the "Norms on the use of Eucharistic Prayers I-IV."[130]

Eucharistic Prayer I, the longest of the four, remains the "primary" prayer, in that it may always be used and is "particularly suited to days assigned to feasts of the apostles and saints; also, to Sundays." It is the longest and most ancient of prayers, being quoted by Saint Ambrose in the mid-300s. Eucharistic Prayer II, the shortest of the four, can be traced back to Hippolytus in the fourth century. Because of its particular features, it is more suited to weekdays. Eucharistic Prayer III is the only one that is not based on an ancient source but instead is a new composition. It is particularly suited for Sundays. Eucharistic Prayer IV is adapted from several Eastern liturgical sources and is considered the most ecumenical of the Eucharistic Prayers. Although it proclaims in more detail than the others the account of salvation history, there is great sensitivity to its use because of the many references to "man." And although their origins may differ and their wording may be unique, the words of concentration are the same in each. The parts of each are the same. They all begin with a thanksgiving (preface) and conclude with a doxology.

Again, to stress the "bottom line," regardless of their antiquity; regardless of their length; and regardless of their "orientation," ***they all have but one purpose: enable the re-presentation of the sacrifice of Calvary to be made present.***

THE PREFACE

The preface,[131] with which the Eucharistic Prayer begins, can be likened to the prelude that the composer of an overture uses to prepare his

---

[130] Father Cassian Folsom proposes six reasons for the change: advances in liturgical studies; dissatisfaction with the Roman Canon and architectural functionalism; the zeitgeist of the late Sixties; theological shift to the "horizontal"; the vernacular and variety; a new formalism. For an in-depth explanation of each, see Ibid pp. 12-15

[131] Because prefaces have the specific purpose of exposing us to what will follow, in terms of the theme for which the Mass is oriented, there is no one preface for all. In fact, where there were 84 prefaces found in the Roman Missal in 1975. Today, there are 156 prefaces available for use by the celebrant. Anthony Ward, SM and Cuthbert Johnson, OSB. "Prefaces of the Roman Missal." October 19, 2008, fontesliturgicae.blogspot.com.

listeners for what they will hear or to the prologue that an author uses to prepare their readers for what is coming up. However, although similar in purpose, the preface is radically different in essence. Whereas, on the one hand, thanks are given for the opportunity to listen to the opera or read what is written in the novel, in the preface, we give thanks for ***the experience of participating*** in the events that will take place in the Mass. Rather than being asked to *react* to the experience of and give thanks for the rewards received from our listening or reading, we are challenged by the preface to be *proactive*. To give thanks for the unmerited opportunity to truly participate in the sacrifice of Calvary re-presented through the actions of the priest acting *in persona christi.*

And as does the composer of the overture or the author of the novel prepare us for what to expect, so does the Divine Composer, who is to offer Himself in sacrifice, prepare us for that which is to take place at His altar through the words of the Preface. But here, He is exposing us to the reality that for all of us who participate in the Mass, it is *an experience, not a performance*. So, as we enter into the events to take place in the Eucharistic Prayer, we are called, through our participation in the preface, to examine our disposition and our commitment as to how it is we will "actively, and consciously participate in the events that will take place." For it is here that Saint Thomas Aquinas calls it "the part of the consecration" dedicated to "exciting the people to devotion."[132] The preface does this by first engaging us in a dialogue, through the invitation of the priest, where we are encouraged to "lift up our hearts to the Word" and "give Him thanks" for what it is we are about to experience. And in responding, we are challenged to recognize than by our doing so, "it is right and just" for the reasons that the priest will then articulate.[133] We then add our thanks using the words given to us by the angels, as we proclaim "Holy, Holy, Holy, Lord."[134] An acclamation by which we "join all of creation in giving thanks to the Father through Christ."[135]

---

[132] Saint Thomas Aquinas, as quoted in Johnson, Eric., "The Preface of the Mass, Giving Thanks to the Lord." spiritualdirection.com, February 7, 2014.

[133] E.g., for the saints and martyrs who will join us in this experience.

[134] Cf. Isaiah 6:3.

[135] Johnson J., Lawrence. *The Mystery of Faith: A Study of the Structural Elements of the Mass.* Federation of Diocesan Liturgical Commissions, Revised Edition, 2003, p. 81.

Thus, it is through the preface that we are given the explanation of what follows in the Eucharistic Prayer, which, if we truly open our hearts and minds to, will enable us to not only prepare for, but gain a "deeper attitude of thanksgiving and praise,"[136] allowing us to better pray the Mass; this will give us a fuller appreciation of what it is we are about to experience.

The stage is now set. The preparations are made. We now prepare for the re-presentation of the sacrifice of Calvary by invoking the assistance of the Holy Spirit. We do this through the prayer known as the *"epiclesis."* A prayer by which we "call upon" or "invoke" the Holy Spirit to enable the offering presented in the Mass to become the body and blood of the One in whose name the sacrifice of the Mass is offered.

THE EPICLESIS

Here, we are calling upon the *same Spirt* who was found to be hovering over the waters that God made through His Word, thus bringing life and order to the world (cf. Genesis 1:1-2). The *same Spirit* who came upon Mary, enabling her to conceive the child who would be called "holy, the Son of God" (cf. Luke 1: 31-34). The *same Spirit* who would descend upon Him at His baptism, revealing through the Father's word that "this is [His] Beloved Son, with whom He was well pleased" (cf. Mark 1:9-11). The *same Spirit* who "cast a shadow over Him" as He was transfigured, and from which the Father commanded us to "listen to Him" (cf. Mark 9:2-8). The *same Spirit* who came upon the apostles at Pentecost, enabling them to proclaim the good news (cf. Acts 2: 2-4). The *same Spirit* who came upon us at our baptism so that we could become "a new creature," an adopted [child] of God who has become a "partaker of the divine nature," a member of Christ and coheir with him and *a temple of the Holy Spirit* (emphasis stressed) (CCC 1265), "no longer [belonging] to [them]self, but to him who died and rose for us" (1269). And as we prepare for this event to take place, this might be a good time for us to pause and ask ourselves, here in terms of our relation with the Holy Spirit, which is the manifestation of God's love, if we

---

136 "Explanation of the Mass – The Preface." homeofthemother.org

have become a "new creature" in terms of our commitment to the One into whose body we are incorporated. Do we truly reflect the truth that we are "temples of the Holy Spirit" in terms of the dignity with which we carry ourselves?

For this is the ***same Spirit*** that the priest, acting *in persona christi,* asks the Father to send "to make holy" (EP II, III) or "sanctify" (EP IV) the gifts of bread and wine "so that they may become the Body and Blood of the Lord."[137] A moment at which the Church manifestly "assert[s] its belief in the divinity of the Holy Spirit."[138] But it does more. In publicly invoking the Hoy Spirit, we make manifest our realization of what Cardinal Wuerl points out: "The gifts cannot be transformed by any human means, but only by the power of God. The Epiclesis makes eminently clear that the Mass is primarily a work of God and not simply a pious action or human custom. Without the power of the Holy Spirit, the Cardinal goes on to state that "the Mass would not be the Mass."[139] This is a reality, however, that seems to escape the majority of Catholics. It is a primary reason why so few Catholics attend Mass.[140] It is for many, I contend, not a sacrificial encounter with the Risen Christ,[141] which in reality it is, but merely, at one end of the spectrum, a spiritual exercise and, at the other end, a social gathering.

Be that as it may, this invocation of the Holy Spirit, which takes place prior to the consecration of the bread and wine into the body and blood of Christ, is not the only time during the Eucharistic Prayer that the Holy Spirit is asked to intercede for us. In this first instance, we are

---

[137] Johnson J., Lawrence. *The Mystery of Faith: A Study of the Structural Elements of the Mass.* Federation of Diocesan Liturgical Commissions, Revised Edition, 2003, p. 83. It is of interest to note that in the Orthodox churches, the epiclesis completes the consecration. In Catholic theology, the Words of Institution (or anamnesis, for those of you starved for Greek terms) are consecratory.

[138] Oury, p. 101.

[139] Wuerl, Donald Cardinal. *The Mass.* Doubleday, New York, 2011, p. 157.

[140] The PEW Research Center survey of July 2020 notes that Mass attendance has dropped from 70% in 1960 to about 20% today.

[141] More on this below when we talk of the transformation of the bread and wine into the body, blood, soul and divinity of Christ in the sections on the institution narrative, the consecration, and the Communion Rite.

asking of the Holy Spirit that the gifts become the body, blood, soul, and divinity of Jesus. After the consecration, the Holy Spirit is once more invoked so that "all be brought together in unity" (EP II), "become one body, one spirit in Christ" (EP III), so that "all who share the bread and wine" be gathered "into the one Body of Christ, a living sacrifice of praise" (EP IV).[142] When you stop and think about it, it makes sense in that the sanctification of the faithful is one of the primary goals of the Eucharist, which by the Holy Spirit will be made present through the words of consecration said by the priest, acting *in persona christi* in the institution narrative and consecration.

THE INSTITUTION NARRATIVE AND CONSECRATION

We have been engaged in the hour from the beginning of Mass. Whatever our disposition has been up to now, we find ourselves here at the **moment**. The moment when the will of the Father is to be consummated. The moment for which Jesus came. The moment by which all He has done and said during His public ministry will be brought together. The moment where He will atone not only for the sin of Adam, but the sins of all mankind, past, present, and future until He comes again. The moment, unlike His baptism, where His Sonship was revealed; unlike His transfiguration, where His purpose for becoming man was revealed. The moment where He now gives us personally, intimately, and timelessly the means by which to succeed in undertaking our particular call to vocation, whether as clergy, religious, or lay. The moment by which we are given the means to bring glory to His Father, His Presence to the world, and the experience of the love of the Holy Spirit to all our discipleship brings us into contact with.

This is the moment by which we find ourselves, as did the apostles at the Last Supper, experiencing the fruits of the Mass. The moment we are asked to look at the depth of our preparation for this experience by looking at how He prepared for the experience. The moment we realize that Jesus, in anticipating the Passover meal He desired to eat with His apostles, understood not only the significance of but the need

---

[142] Johnson, p. 83.

to prepare for it. The moment where we find Him giving His disciples specific instructions as to how they were to prepare for the event (cf. Matthew 26:17-19). The moment where we find them going off and finding everything exactly as He had told them (cf. Luke 22:7-13). The moment when the supper began and He took His place at the table with His apostles, telling them, as He is telling us who are at the Table of the Eucharist (the Altar), that "[He] *eagerly desires* (italics stressed) to eat this Passover with them" (cf. Luke 22: 15-16). A desire that remains unabated to this day, **which is why He asks us to spend this, His hour with Him**. This is not only done to give us His body and blood, as He did His apostles then, but to let us know of just how much He longs for having a genuine and intimate relationship with us now.[143]

Thus, the apostles, in anticipation of the perfect sacrifice of Calvary, and, we through the re-presentation of that same sacrifice, are asked to prepare ourselves for that experience. An experience by which we "enter into a future that He has already achieved and established where all things in heaven and on earth are recapitulated in Him" [a moment where] "we are already standing forever with the angels in heaven."[144] The question for those who were with Him then, as it is for us who are with Him today, is to reflect on how it is we have prepared for our encountering Him. And we can do so by looking at the way we participate in the Holy Sacrifice of the Mass. They in the presence of Jesus in His humanity, we in the presence of the priest, acting *in persona christi*. The priest, who *in persona christi*, will give us in the bread offered, His body, and in the wine offered, His blood. The moment where the bread and wine become mysteriously and sacramentally **His real body and His real blood**. The body and blood willingly offered up by Jesus on the Cross of Calvary, albeit here in the Mass in an unbloody manner, by which His **Glorified Body** becomes truly present.

The moment when we, who are at the Mass, are asked to look at the priest (as he acts *in persona christi*) as he lifts up the wafer of unleavened

---

[143] This theme is based on Msgr. Peter J. Vaghi's article "Preparing the Upper Room. Franciscan Spirit Blog February 7, 2017.

[144] Driscoll, Jeremy, OSB. *What Happens at Mass.* Gracewing Publishing, 2005, p. 73.

wheat bread, saying the words of consecration; it is here we can truly see the body of the Glorified Jesus who is truly present under what now is merely the appearance of bread. To truly see the One who is to be lifted up on the cross to be sacrificed for the many. Then, in the same way, the priest, once again acting *in persona christi,* raises the chalice containing the wine made from the grape and once more speaks the words of consecration; again, we truly see the One who willingly offers up His blood for us, which is really present under the appearances of wine.

And by doing so at the Last Supper, we find that Jesus, a priest of the order of Melchizedek (cf. Psalm 110; Hebrews 7:17), also offers us the sacrifice of the Mass (by anticipation at the Last Supper) under the form of bread and wine as did Melchizedek (cf. Genesis 14:18).[145] This He did, as the fathers at the council noted, "in order *to perpetuate the sacrifice of the cross throughout the centuries until he should come again,* and so to entrust to his beloved spouse, the Church, *a memorial of his death and resurrection: a sacrament of love, a sign of unity, a bond of charity, a paschal banquet in which Christ is consumed, the mind is filled with grace,* and *a pledge of future glory is given to us.*"[146]

The moment then, where, if we stop and think about what we are experiencing, find ourselves encountering three events that I proclaim are miracles.[147] The first is the incarnation (or coming into existence in the world) of the Glorified Christ, who will be offered up in an unbloodied manner as the sacrifice to be re-presented. He is made truly present, in a mysterious and sacramental way, so that the worthy victim be there to

---

[145] Since Psalm 110 predicted Christ would be a priest "after the order of Melchizedek," that is, offering a sacrifice in bread and wine, it is said that we must look for some sacrifice other than Calvary because it was not under the form of bread and wine. The Mass meets that need.

[146] *Sacrosanctum Concilium* 47.

[147] A *miracle* is defined as an extraordinary sensible effect wrought by God that surpasses the power and order of created by nature. Karlo Broussard points out that there are five aspects to a miracle: 1: Exclusively attributable to divine power; 2. beyond the power of created nature; 3: beyond the order of created nature; 4: extraordinary; and 5: sensible. Broussard, Karlo. "What Constitutes a Miracle." *Catholic Answers,* April 19, 2016.

be sacrificed. The second is that we find ourselves mysteriously present at Calvary, standing with Mary, John, and the Magdalene, witnessing this perfect act of divine love, His sacrifice as it is re-presented on the altar. Then, finally, what Our Lord intended from His words and actions at the first Mass; what He offered to us from His cross; and what we are offered at the Mass—the Eucharist—is made present.[148] The Eucharist being the means by which we are enabled to respond to His requiring us to eat His body and drink His blood. The Eucharist by which we are fed, strengthened, and enabled to live our discipleship in a way that brings glory to His Father, to Him, and the means for experiencing the love of the Holy Spirit. The Eucharist, by which we will have everlasting life (cf. John 6:54).

This is an experience so profound that we now pause to reflect on just what it was that Our Lord, in His unsurpassed love for us, did.

THE ANAMNESIS

We have been witnesses to the consummation of the Father's plan. We have experienced the reality of the perfect sacrifice of the Son, which enabled His Father's plan to be consummated. The sacrifice which was, through the actions of the priest, sacramentally re-presented in an unbloody manner for our redemption. We have been exposed to His real presence made mysteriously present through the words of consecration under the appearances of bread and wine. A presence that will be offered to us in the Sacrament of the Eucharist. These are mysterious realities that require us to pause and reflect on their meaning to us as disciples, which we do through what is known as the anamnesis.[149]

---

[148] Oury points out that according to the definition of the Council of Trent, the authentication of the institution is the author of the Sacrament of the Eucharist. Oury, Guy, Rev. *The Mass.* Catholic Book Publishing Company, New York, 1988, p. 192.

[149] The following approach is based on ideas on the anamnesis given in a talk by Father Kevin Walsh, which he based on Pitre, Brant. *Jesus and the Jewish Roots of the Eucharist: Unlocking the Secrets of the Last Supper.* Image, New York, 2016. The talk was given to the deacons of the Diocese of Arlington at their annual convocation with their bishop on February 5, 2022.

The anamnesis, which is Greek for the Hebrew word *zaked*, which means "remembrance" and means something more than merely referring to the past alone. In the Jewish understanding of the word, it has the meaning of not only the remembrance of an event, but an ***experiencing*** of that event. Quoting Rabbi Lawrence Hoffman (from Pitre's book), Father Walsh points out that "time stops momentarily and the past and the present become the same." This significant point is expanded on by Thomas Griffin, who, in quoting Aristotle, tells us that "the anamnesis is an 'externalizing' of the present into a present of things past, a present of things present, and a present of things future."[150] Because it is in the remembrance of the event as experienced then by the Jews in Passover and we in the holy sacrifice of the Mass that the event is made present. For it is here that we are reminded that the Church is acting "in memory of the Lord" and is "obeying His explicit command 'Do this in memory of me.'"[151] This is a point reinforced by Roguet in stating that it is the offering that is essential to the anamnesis.[152]

Thus, in our experiencing the re-presentation of the sacrifice of Calvary, we find that Christ is mystically present; sacramentally present; and substantially present. Thus, what happened some two thousand years ago on a hill named Calvary is not only remembered, but experienced. A reality that Carl Olson, in citing Orthodox authors, interestingly points out "that the sacrifice re-presented is more true and real for us who relive it 'according to the Spirit' than it was for those who lived it 'according to the flesh,' *before the Holy Spirit revealed the full meaning to the Church*'" (emphasis added).[153]

INTERCESSIONS

We have experienced the sacrifice on Calvary re-presented in an unbloody manner through the words of consecration. We now come

---

[150] Griffin, Thomas. "A Theological, Historical, and Social Study of the Anamnesis in Christian Liturgy." *The Catholic World Report*, May 12, 2021.

[151] Belmonte, Charles. *Understanding the Mass.* Scepter Publications, Princeton, New Jersey, 1997, p. 145.

[152] Roguet, A. M. Rev OP. *The New Mass.* Catholic Book Publishing Company, New York, 1970, p. 135.

[153] Olson, Carl E. "Renewal, Re-presentation, and Anamnesis." *The Catholic World*, April 7, 2012.

to publicly recognize through these intercessions those for whom that sacrifice was offered. These are intercessions by which it is made clear that it is not only for those present at the Mass, but the entire Church of heaven and of earth. Of note is to recognize these intercessions differ from those of the general intercessions offered during the Liturgy of the Word. Whereas those were offered for both members and nonmembers of the Church both on earth and in heaven, these intercessions are focused on Church members only. These intercessions are made "for all her members living and dead."[154] Both by name as well as in general,[155] as seen especially in Eucharistic Prayer I. In that prayer, we find those intercessions offered by name in the first part, oriented to the twelve apostles and twelve martyrs,[156] whereas in the second part, we find eight male and seven female martyrs also identified by name.[157]

These intercessions are usually divided into three sections. One section is devoted to living Christians (as Wuerl notes: for the Pope, the order of bishops, the clergy, and those taking part in the offering[158]); the second part is for the dead (as seen in the recognition of the apostles, the saints, and martyrs); whereas in the third part, it [recognizes] our relation to the saints in heaven, with whom we someday desire to be.[159]

Thus, it is here where, for us who are present to witness this sacrifice, the challenge arises. It is here where we are challenged to look at what our intentions are as these intercessions are offered. We ask ourselves if our desire to be with the saints in union with Him around His Father's table in heaven is genuine and intense, for example, as that of Saint Paul,

---

[154] GIRM No. 78.

[155] Dubruiel, Michael. *The How-To Book of the Mass.* Our Sunday Visitor Huntington, Indiana, 2002, p. 163.

[156] The Apostles Peter and Paul, Andrew, James, John, Thomas, James, Philip, Bartholomew, Matthew, Simon, and Jude. The martyrs Linus, Cletus, Clement, Sixtus, Cornelius, Cyprian, Lawrence, Chrysogonus, John and Paul, Cosmas, and Damian.

[157] John the Baptist, Stephen, Matthias, Barnabas, Ignatius, Alexander, Marcellinus, Peter, Felicity, Perpetua, Agatha, Lucy, Agnes, Cecilia, and Anastasia.

[158] Wuerl, Donald Cardinal. *The Mass.* Doubleday, New York, 2011, p. 174.

[159] Belmonte, Charles. *Understanding the Mass.* Scepter Publications, Princeton, New Jersey, 1997, p. 153.

who wanted nothing less than "to know Christ and the power of his resurrection and the sharing of his sufferings by becoming like Him in His death, if somehow, I may attain the resurrection from the dead."[160] Or are our intentions like those of His disciples, when challenged by Him to do what we are about to do, through the Sacrament of the Eucharist, eat His flesh and drink His blood, finding our desire to also "fall short" of that mark, for whatever reason? Remembering as we ponder this challenge, as pointed our earlier, the faith and devotion by which we do so, *is known to Him*.

THE DOXOLOGY

We have come full circle. What we started the Eucharistic Prayer with, we now end with. Where we began with our recognition that "Heaven and earth are full of [the Father's] glory," we now reiterate that truth by recognizing through the priest's acclamation that "all glory and honor is [again due the Father]" in what is known as the *doxology* (from the Greek word for *"praise"*).[161] We now find ourselves coming to the close of the Eucharistic Prayer. But with a difference. Whereas we proclaimed His glory at the beginning of the prayer as one body present at the Mass during the "Holy, Holy, Holy," now, we are exposed to the recognition of the Father's glory through the words of the priest who informs us that that glory is rendered "through [Jesus, the one whose sacrifice we experienced re-presented], and with Him, and in Him."[162] A glory that is given the Father through the Son and rendered in the unity of the Holy Spirit.[163] For it is in the Holy Spirit that the Church finds its unity and communion, as well as its sanctification through the indwelling of

---

[160] Philippians 3:10-11.

[161] The word doxology as an expression of praise to God, usually liturgical. This word is comprised of the Greek words *doxa* and *logos*. In the Greek language, doxa means glory, splendor, or grandeur, while the Greek word logos means word or speaking. Merriam-Webster.com\dictionary

[162] The form of the doxology that Oury notes is found to be a combination of several scripture passages: Rom 16:27, 1Tim1:17, Gal 1:5, and Jude 25. Oury, Guy, Rev. *The Mass.* Catholic Book Publishing Company, New York, 1988, p. 102.

[163] Ibid. p. 103.

the Spirit. The means by which she, through her members, can, through their words and actions, also render all honor and glory to the Father.

What is of more importance, however, is for us to stop and ponder how this glory in rendered by Christ. If we listen closely to the prayer of the priest, we can recognize that this glory is given not only by Christ, but by us as well. Think about it. True, the glory is given "through Him," as well it should be, but it is also given "with Him" and "in Him." We give it "through Him" because He said to us that "no one can come to the Father except through Him" (cf. John 14:6). For us to have access to His Father, we must be one with Him in the sacrifice that had just been offered. This is a reality acknowledged by the priest when he asks that not only His sacrifice, but *ours,* be accepted. Thus, the reason for us stating that "all glory and honor is the Father's." For in doing so, we are publicly acknowledging our recognition of the Father's glory. But it's important to note that we also render the Father's glory *with* Our Lord. Why? Because He tells us (cf. John 15:5) that "without Him we can do nothing but *with Him* all things are possible." Yet our rendering the Father's glory doesn't stop there. We render His glory *in* Our Lord. Because it is only through "eating His flesh and drinking His blood" that we can truly "live in Him and He can live in [us] (cf. John 6:56). [164]

Thus, we are at the moment when prior to our confirming "Amen," we find ourselves in the presence of the Risen and Gloried Lord. No longer is there anything that stands between us and the Risen Christ sacramentally present before us. His sacrifice has been accepted by the Father as proof for all eternity as the perfect, unrepeatable sacrifice by which the sin of Adam, as well as ours and all others, have been atoned for; our redemption has been accomplished, and entry once more into the Kingdom of the Father has been made accessible. However, once again, we find ourselves faced with the question as to where it is we are at this moment. Are we continuing to "pass by" the now Glorified Lord standing before us as He was earlier in His crucified body? Are we

---

[164] The above discussion is based on the discussion put forth by Belmonte. Belmonte, Charles. *Understanding the Mass.* Scepter Publications, Princeton, New Jersey, 1997, p. 162.

continuing to "standoff" from Him to see what may transpire? Or, like the Magdalene on that first Sunday morning, do we want to rush and grab onto Him in an intimate and loving embrace? This is an opportunity we will next be presented with in the Communion Rite, which will begin after our "Amen," bringing the Eucharistic Prayer to a close.

But here again, this is not just any "Amen." No! According to Driscoll, this is the "biggest Amen of the Mass and so is the biggest Amen in the world. [It is] an Amen that never ends."[165] It can be said[166] to be "both a prayer (of our hope in the resurrection) and a resolution (to see that the love given us in the Holy Spirit blossoms)." It is an "Amen" that announces in no uncertain terms that we not only are certain that what happened truly occurred but that "we approve!" An "Amen" that is our public offering of thanks for the Father's acceptance of the bread and wine, which through the words of consecration became the body and blood of Christ. An "Amen" that proclaims, "That it is time!"[167] Time to come face to face with Our Risen Lord in the most intimate moment of the Mass—our entering into the Communion Rite, where we will be afforded the privilege of communion with Him in the Sacrament of the Eucharist. The time to prepare ourselves, in terms of our "faith and devotion," to enter into a genuine encounter with the Risen Jesus at the moment of our communion with Him in the Sacred Species offered to us in His name by His ministers.

---

[165] Driscoll, Jeremy, OSB. *What Happens at Mass.* Gracewing Publishing, 2005, pp. 107–108.

[166] Belmonte, Charles. *Understanding the Mass.* Scepter Publications, Princeton, New Jersey, 1997, p. 163.

[167] Roguet, A. M. Rev OP. *The New Mass.* Catholic Book Publishing Company, New York, 1970, p. 153.

CHAPTER FOUR: THE COMMUNION RITE

THE OUR FATHER

The sacrifice has been offered and accepted. The purpose for which the Son of Man became man has been accomplished. Sin has been conquered. Death has forever lost its sting. We who have just witnessed these events re-presented through the words of consecration are now given not only the opportunity, but the unmerited privilege of sharing in His glorified life through the Eucharist. But in doing so, we are also challenged to recognize that it is not merely His life we share in, but that of those present at the Mass and, more significantly, those we encounter after leaving the Mass.

However, first, we first must stop and remind ourselves as to what communion with the Risen Lord entails. To help us in our efforts to do so, Jesus doesn't merely suggest, but **commands,** us to pray. He goes further. He **dares** us to pray. To pray in a way that the entire gamut of what discipleship entails is articulated. Yet Jesus, in recognizing our limitations, once again comes to our aid. He teaches us how to pray. Not from a merely human or historical or even theological perspective, but from His perspective, a divine perspective. In a mere sixty-six words, He gives us the prayer we know as the Our Father. A prayer that encourages us to realize that it is to the Father that we are called to pray. A prayer by which we will personally and publicly commit to recognizing all that the Father has done and will do for us. A prayer that will enable us to not only embrace, but truly commune with His Son. A prayer that enables us to recognize that as disciples, we are called to "hallow His name." That to do so, we must not only enable His "kingdom to come," but also that His "will be done on earth as it is in heaven." A prayer that is truly the summary of the whole Gospel" (CCC 2761). A prayer that, by praying it *and living it,* will lead us toward saintliness, for as Mother Teresa notes, "The Our Father contains everything: God, ourselves, our neighbors...." A prayer, however, that also presents us with a challenge. To have the courage to ask ourselves, "What *is* His will for me?" Here again, we find Jesus coming to our assistance. He shows us by example in the garden that His Father's will for us may also transcend our human perspective and may not necessarily be known or recognized in tangible ways. That we, too, despite what we may perceive from human experience, are called upon to subordinate that experience by faith in allowing His will to be done to us. This is an effort that we are asked to realize that can only be achieved by our total dependence on Him. We can do this by admitting that He is the One who gives us each day, what it is we need to succeed in living our discipleship as He desires. This challenges us to recognize that as disciples, we too, as was Jesus, also will be exposed to temptations. Temptations that we will find to intensify in direct relationship to how committed we are to our particular living our particular vocation. Yet we also recognize that although temptations in themselves are not sinful, they can, if we allow them to, lead us to sin.[168] But the Our Father is a prayer by which we acknowledge the Father's steadfast love for us as manifested in His unwavering offer of mercy. It is a prayer by which we recognize that we will, at times, fall. And because of that reality, we realize that it is He whom we must ask to deliver us from the evil caused by our sins. But this is where the "rubber meets the road." For although the Father's commitment to us is unconditional, we must recognize what our commitment to the Father is. It is a commitment on our part that takes on great significance in our recognition that we are sinners. That as sinners, we depend on the Father's forgiveness. And by seeking the Father's forgiveness, we commit to Him by our response that we profess that we are willing to accept the level and degree of His forgiveness of

---

[168] An example of how temptation can lead to sinful thoughts was given to us during our diaconal formation. It was a story of two friars walking along a path leading to a river. As they approached the river, they met a lady who was in distress that she could not cross it by herself. One of the friars offered to carry her across by putting her on his back, after which they went across. At the opposite shore, the friar put the lady down, and the two friars went on their way. About a mile down the path, the other friar said to the one who carried the lady across that it was scandalous of him to put the lady on his back. The friar responded, "I left her back at the river's bank. You seem to be still carrying her."

us, as we forgive those who sin against us. This is a challenge whose seed can be found planted by Jesus in asking of us, who wishes to be known as His disciples, to live His new commandment that we love others as He loves us. It is a challenge that can be traced back to Our Lord's admonition that we go to our brother first to deal with his sins before we come to meet Him at the altar, from which we will receive Him in the Eucharist.[169]

THE SIGN OF PEACE

We now find ourselves at the point in the Mass where our anticipation of meeting the Risen Lord is at its peak. At the same time, however, we find ourselves in the "shoes," so to speak, of the apostles who encountered the Risen Lord for the first time. Somewhat apprehensive (as those in the upper room that first Easter Sunday), maybe even doubtful (as was Thomas in the face of the reality of His being risen), or startled (as was the Magdalene in the garden) because the presence of the Risen Lord appears to them as someone other than what they expected He would look like. This is an experience that caused them to not recognize the Jesus they knew, followed, and loved during His earthly ministry as He appeared in His glorified body. A challenge similar to the one faced by those at the Mass in recognizing this same Jesus, in His glorified body standing before them under the appearances of bread and wine in the Eucharist.

Recognizing this dissonance among His apostles, as he does among us now, He reaches out once again, to offer us, as He did them, His peace! Yet it is not the same peace that the world offers (cf. John 14:27). No! This peace, His peace, is a peace by which we are enabled to not only face up to, but endure all the turmoil, troubles, challenges, rejections, sufferings, or persecutions our discipleship will bring us. This is a peace that, since its origins, comes from the Son of God, and is a permanent and everlasting peace, unlike that of the world, which is fleeting and temporary. It is a peace that surpasses all understanding (cf. Phil 4:7).

---

[169] Matthew 18:15-18.

A peace that does not promise comfort or ease. A peace that does not remove the effects of worldly experiences. But it is a peace that will give us the confidence to do His will, knowing that He will always be present, going before us on our particular path of discipleship. A peace that will enable us, as Paul promises in his 1st Letter to the Corinthians, to recognize that He will not allow us to be tried beyond what we are able to deal with, but in the face of whatever we find ourselves facing in living our discipleship, will provide us the way to overcome those trials successfully (cf. 1 Cor 10:13). A peace that will enable us to recognize that His grace will be all we need to deal successfully with whatever weaknesses, insults, hardships, difficulties, or persecutions our discipleship brings us (cf. 2 Cor 12:9-10).

Yet it is a peace that must not be possessed: it must be shared. This is a challenge presented to us when the deacon asks us to offer that peace to our brethren at Mass. That we have the courage of our faith in His peace given to us, that we can, in turn, do so in some manner that proclaims it is not only His peace, but our peace as well. For it is in the manner and with the intention that we offer that peace that we will experience the depth of that blessedness that the Risen Lord promises His peace to us who do so (cf. Matt 5:9).

THE FRACTION

We are now ready to recognize the reality of the Risen Lord's presence among us under the appearances of the bread and wine. The One with whom we will soon commune. And to do so, the priest, taking the consecrated Host, **breaks it**[170] to symbolize the "image of the Lord's body on the cross being 'broken' in order to give us life, to be distributed to us."[171] After doing so, the priest then takes a piece of the broken Host and places it in the chalice as a symbolic "reenactment of the Lord's

---

[170] The fraction, or the breaking of the bread, is what the Eucharist was called in the early church (cf. Acts 2:42). It is interesting to note, as Belmonte points out, that the Jews always *broke*, never *cut*, the bread. Belmonte, Charles. *Understanding the Mass.* Scepter Publications, Princeton, New Jersey, 1997, p. 177.

[171] Driscoll, Jeremy, OSB. *What Happens at Mass.* Gracewing Publishing, 2005, p. 124.

resurrection, by which, in overcoming death, His Body and Blood are one again."[172] In this action, the priest accomplishes two things. First, it links us with Jesus because "the bread we break" will be the means by which we are able to "partake of the Body of Our Lord." But it also proclaims the meaning of our unity, our oneness. Because although we are many, by "partaking of the one bread, we are one body" (cf. 1 Cor 10:16-17).[173]

A oneness, a unity that in the early Church, through the fraction rite that was symbolized by two traditions. One originating with Pope Innocent I in the fifth century. The other by the actions of the priest to recognize that no matter how many, when, or where the Holy Sacrifice of the Mass is celebrated, it was really one Mass, one Sacrifice offered for believers in the whole Church. The first, where Pope Innocent, taking fragments of the Host he consecrated, sends them by acolytes to the pastors of the churches in Rome, symbolizing that all the masses celebrated in Rome were really one Mass. The second being when a priest, having celebrated Mass, would leave a fragment of the Host he consecrated on the altar for use by the next priest celebrating Mass at that altar. The action was meant to symbolize that all masses were really the one Mass, the one Sacrifice.[174]

Having now recognized publicly through the fraction and comingling the presence of the Risen Lord, the priest now presents Him to those present. He does so by holding up the sacramental species of bread and wine and **challenges us,** as did Pilate on that fateful Friday morning, to **behold!** Behold Him who under Pilate's command was crucified and who, at the will of the Father, rose again on the third day. We are challenged to behold Him who takes away the sins of the world. To behold Him who is now calling for us to join with Him at His supper. And as He stands before us under the sacramental species

---

[172] Johnson J., Lawrence. *The Mystery of Faith: A Study of the Structural Elements of the Mass.* Federation of Diocesan Liturgical Commissions, Revised Edition, 2003, p. 105.
[173] Roguet, A. M. Rev OP. *The New Mass.* Catholic Book Publishing Company, New York, 1970, pp. 162–163.
[174] Irwin, Kevin W. Response to 101 Questions on the Mass. Paulist Press, New York/Mahwah, New Jersey, 1999, pp. 124–125.

and as we look upon Him, we are asked to reflect on the reality that we are "not worthy" to enter into an experience so sacred, so intimate, so life changing. But this is not a self-condemnation. No! It is a challenge to realize the wish of the Risen Lord for us to become all we were created in love to be. To be "perfect as the Father is perfect" (cf. Matt 5:48). Perfect in the sense that Paula Gooder, in looking at the original Greek word *teleoous*, gives us insights as to what Our Lord was asking of us. Using the Greek translation, she points out that what He is really asking of us is to be "rounded," be "whole," be "complete" in who we are.[175] To recognize His ardent desire to enter into communion with us (cf. Luke 22:15). And because of our recognition of His desire and our unworthiness to do so, we ask of Him that He "but say the word." Why? Because it was by His Word that the blind saw, the lame walked, the sick were healed, and the dead were raised. Which is why we ask of Him to but say the word, however damaged by sin, uncertainty, doubt ,or even disbelief,[176] so that, by His doing so, "our soul will be healed!"

This is a challenge that asks us to pause and consider, "How strong is our commitment to truly offer Him our soul to be healed?" "How confident are we at this moment of anticipation of being worthy to commune with Him in the Sacrament by which He awaits us?" Will we have the faith of the centurion and truly give Him our soul to heal unconditionally, or will we be like the rich young man and find it too hard to do? This is an answer that will determine the preparedness, the desire that we will bring with us as we approach Him in the sacrament.

COMMUNION

The time has arrived. The fruit of His sacrifice offered on Calvary and re-presented at the Mass—the Eucharist—is not only ready to be approached, but to be consumed. We are now presented with the unmerited privilege to witness that reality in the Host held high by the

---

[175] Paula Gooder. "Behold the Lamb of God." biblestudy.org.vic, September 22, 2016.

[176] Bishop Barron, in his video on YouTube, citing the latest PEW report, states that less than 25% of Catholics believe in the Christ's real presence in the Eucharist.

priest. By doing so, what the priest is challenging us is to **behold**! To behold **Him**. Behold Him who through His passion, death, resurrection, and ascension "**took away the sins of the world**." But as He "stands before us," offering Himself to us in unconditional love, we are also challenged to reflect on our own offer of ourselves to Him in this communion. To reflect on our "worthiness" to become one with Him in our reception of the Eucharist. To look at where we are in our relationship with Him. To recall once again[177] what we "have done or failed to do" in terms of enabling our relationship with Him to thrive. Then and only then can we see if we have the courage to recognize that, to whatever degree and for whatever reason, we have "come up short"; that we "are not worthy" to receive Him in the Eucharist. Yet in the face of that recognition, we are once again asked to look at the faith of our conviction in His love for us. A faith that allows us to hear His response to our confession of unworthiness. To hear that because of His love of us, because of His mercy toward us, He is willing, if we but ask Him to "say the word" that will enable us to worthily receive Him in the Eucharist. His "imprimatur" will allow those of us who find ourselves in a state of grace to approach Him worthily.

To experience the moment when we and He became one sacramentally. A moment so simple yet so profound. A moment when the minister of Holy Communion presents Him under the appearances of bread and wine.[178] A reality that we attest to in our "Amen." This is an Amen by which we publicly profess our membership in His body, the Church, as well as our belief in all the truths held and taught by that same Church. But here, we are challenged "to stand tall!"; "to stand firm!"; "to stand resolute!" in our proclamation that our

---

[177] As we did in our praying the Confiteor earlier.

[178] Recognizing, as the Catechism points out, that **Christ** is sacramentally (and equally) present **under each species;** therefore, if a person receives only one species, Christ is fully present, and nothing is lacking.

Amen professes *He is truly present, body, blood, soul, and divinity in the Eucharist* we receive, whether on the tongue or in the hand.[179]

However, the journey doesn't end there. No! We now find ourselves challenged by this profound and mysterious encounter to reflect on what just happened: what our communion with the Risen Lord means for us as His disciples. And here, I contend that in this life, one cannot, within the limitations of our humanity, fully understand this experience of communing with Our Lord outside of the Sacrament of Marriage, where the "two become one." Yet even in this most intimate act of communion between a husband and wife, one cannot but get a glimpse of what happens at the moment of communion. A glimpse that will only become clear when we experience the Beatific Vision. This is a reality that

---

[179] The Sacred Congregation for Divine Worship, in the document *Memoriale Domini*, offers this brief history of Communion on the tongue: "Later, with a deepening understanding of the truth of the eucharistic mystery, of its power and of the presence of Christ in it, there came a greater feeling of reverence towards this sacrament and a deeper humility was felt to be demanded when receiving it. Thus, the custom was established of the minister placing a particle of consecrated bread on the tongue of the communicant" (*Instruction on the Manner of Distributing Holy Communion, Memoriale Domini*).

This practice arose because of an increased devotion to Christ in the Blessed Sacrament. Placing the Eucharist directly on the communicant's tongue lessened the need for the recipient's hands to be clean, protected the Eucharist from being taken home for superstitious reasons or profane use, and reduced the possibility of crumbs falling to the floor. It wasn't until the 1960s that some episcopal conferences requested permission from the Holy See to once again place the consecrated host directly in the hands of the faithful. Permission for administering Communion in the hand was granted by the Holy See to the United States on June 17, 1977, and has since become almost the universal norm in the Ordinary Form. Today, both manners of receiving Communion are worthy and licit. Whether to receive Communion in the hand or on the tongue are liturgical disciplines, not dogmas. The Church instructs that it is up to the communicant to decide the preferred manner. Neither is more or less noble. What is of most importance is that the communicant be in a state of grace and wishes to be united to Christ through Holy Communion. Gonzalez, Dan. "Communion: in the Hand or the Tongue." Archdiocese of Miami webpage, June 14, 2021.

we experience that challenges us to look not only at our commitment at that moment, however genuine it may be, but at His commitment to us in His giving to us under sacramental signs His entire self.

This is why the Church asks of us to spend a moment of silence after our communion with Him. To realize the impact of our having just been given not merely an opportunity, but the unmerited privilege, of sharing our experience of being one with Him through our reception of the Eucharist. An experience we are challenged to share not only with our brothers and sisters at the Mass, but all those we will encounter upon leaving the Mass. An opportunity that is articulated (albeit, silently) by the deacon (or the priest) in the purification of the vessels after communion. A prayer by which we ask the Lord that "***What has passed our lips as food, O Lord, may we possess in purity of heart, that what has been given to us in time, may be our healing for eternity.***" It is a prayer that we who have just received Our Lord are challenged to see if they, too, each in their own way, have faith enough in Him and in His Sacrament to say that prayer as well.

PRAYER AFTER COMMUNION

We have met the Risen Lord in the Eucharist. We have just communed with Him in the Sacrament. We now pause to silently reflect, knowing in faith that the experience transcends our ability to fully comprehend what has just happened. Now is the time for us to acknowledge that the gifts of Christ's body and blood will "exert their positive effects on all who have received them."[180] The effects which will enable us, through our words and deeds, to share the fruits of our experiences at Mass with the world in which we carry out our discipleship.

---

[180] Champlin, Joseph M. *The Mystery and Meaning of the Mass.* The Crossword Publishing Company, New York, 1998, p. 119.

To recognize this reality, the priest now calls us to prayer.[181] A prayer petitioning the Father, through Christ, and the Holy Spirit that the mystery just celebrated will strengthen our hope of attaining heaven; reinforce our commitment to live what we celebrated; experience more fully the gift of salvation received; and be more willing to not only recognize but welcome Christ in the way we treat others.[182]

It is a prayer that has two parts or objectives: to recall the gift we have just received and to petition that this gift may produce its fruits in us. However, this is not a prayer of thanksgiving but a prayer "asking for the spiritual effects or fruits of the Eucharist" to be realized.[183] Not now, but in the world we will soon reenter upon our going from the Mass.

---

[181] A prayer that first appeared in the fifth century where it was called the "prayer at the conclusion." Johnson J., Lawrence. *The Mystery of Faith: A Study of the Structural Elements of the Mass.* Federation of Diocesan Liturgical Commissions, Revised Edition, 2003, p. 124.

[182] Irwin, Kevin W. *Response to 101 Questions on the Mass.* Paulist Press, New York/Mahwah, New Jersey, 1999, p. 139.

[183] Roguet, A. M. Rev OP. *The New Mass.* Catholic Book Publishing Company, New York, 1970, p. 181.

CHAPTER FIVE: THE CONCLUDING RITE

THE FINAL BLESSING

Consummatum est! It is finished. We have left the Table of the Word, where we were nourished by the teachings of the Lord. We have left the Table of the Eucharist, where we were strengthened by the Eucharist, the Bread of Life.[184] Now, we must go. We must go, as did Mary, John, and the Magdalene, from the hill of Calvary to share with others the events they experienced. We too must as disciples go and take what we have heard from the Scriptures and experienced in our communion with the Risen and Glorified Lord through the Eucharist, sharing those experiences with others.

However, before we go, Jesus, through His priest, wants us to be certain of two things. First, that He *will* be with us, no matter where our discipleship takes us as we leave the Mass and return to the world in which we live. But not in any random way or manner. No! He tells us that as we live our particular call to discipleship, whether as clergy, religious, or laity, *He will go before us*! To show us by His Presence, through His graces, and by His love that He will never lead us astray. He will always point us in the direction that leads to His Father's banquet table. Yet having experienced through His public ministry everything we have, with the exception of sin, He recognizes first hand that we cannot do it alone. So the second thing He gives us through His priest before we go is His blessing. The blessing by which we are given the graces needed to do what it is He will ask of us, as He did His apostles.

Then and only then does He, this time through His deacon, as He did His disciples at His Ascension, send us forth to *proclaim the good news*. To reveal all that He has said and done. Again, we have specific instructions.

---

[184] For more on this concept of the "two tables," see Oury, Guy, Rev. *The Mass*. Catholic Book Publishing Company, New York, 1988, p. 58.

First, that we *go in peace*. Not necessarily a comforting peace, but a peace that will enable us, as it did the apostles that first Easter Sunday, to do His will in confidence. The confidence in His assurance that wherever our journey of discipleship will take us, whatever the experiences our discipleship will bring us, we will have the capability of living them successfully if we but make the effort to do so. Why? Because when He asks us, again through His deacon, *to "glorify [Him] by [the Way we live our] lives,*[185] we need to know how we are asked to do so. Which we learn by His challenging us, as He did His apostles before returning to His Father, to live our discipleship in a way that truly "proclaim[s] the [good news] of the Lord in a way that is not only recognized but accepted by those we meet." That out of love for His Father He became man; that out of love for us He willingly undertook His passion and death to redeem us from the sin of Adam; that through the love of the Holy Spirit who is given us through the love of the Father and the Son, He overcame death by His resurrection and through His ascension prepared a place for us at His Father's banquet table in heaven.

Now, although the Mass *has* ended, it isn't really over. To paraphrase Winston Churchill,[186] while it is in a particular sense "the end of the beginning," it is certainly not yet "the beginning of the end," where we will greet the risen and glorified Jesus as He comes again to judge the living and the dead.[187] Where He will look upon us, His disciples, to discern how it is we have lived our particular call to discipleship. Where He will look at how it was that we not only accepted but carried that particular cross He gave us (Luke 9:23). Did we do so grudgingly? Or reluctantly? Or did we do so willingly, in a way that we emulate Him? Where He will look at how it was that we lived His new commandment (John 13:34)? He will look at how well we have loved, using His love for us as His baseline.

---

[185] An example of why Our Lord asks us to do so can be seen in a story from Ghandi, who was asked by a follower that since he was always quoting Jesus, why he wasn't a Christian. It was said that Ghandi replied, "If I ever met one, I would become one."

[186] Winston Churchill speech to Parliament, November 10, 1942.

[187] Matthew 25:31-36 (cf. 2 Tim 4:1; Rom 14:10).

Will He find that we loved Him, others, and ourselves with the intimacy of wedded spouses? Or the intensity of a grandparent for their grandchild? Or will He find our "love" merely practical or perfunctory? He will look at how we have interacted with Him in those others that our discipleship brings us into contact with (Matthew 25:31-46). The question for us is the question posed in that same Gospel passage: How do we, in our interactions with those we meet in living our particular call to discipleship, not only know that was Him we met, but how we are challenged to treat them? One good way for us to do so is to look at the guidance the Church provides us in its corporal and spiritual works of mercy.[188] This can help in how we interact with others. Which of the works of mercy do we find ourselves undertaking, and more importantly, which of them do we not find ourselves undertaking? Which of them do we find ourselves most comfortable doing? Which of them do we find the most difficulty in doing? The challenge that poses for us, in terms of the reality of His coming again to judge our efforts, is if we will have the courage to accept the graces given to us at the end of Mass and use those graces in a way that we live by those precepts. Particularly those we find it most difficult to practice. What will He find in our actions toward others, particularly those who are unable or unwilling to recognize Him because of preconceived notions as to who among them are needy and what they may need? Will that cause us to not only find ourselves unwilling or reluctant to address their needs, but create an inability to see in them that it is really Him who stands before us? Or will He find us among those, as did Mother Teresa, who were able to recognize not only their needs but see in all those in need, for whatever reason, the Person of Christ standing before us? These are questions that we will find ourselves having to answer when He comes again (cf. Matt 25:45-46).

---

[188] The spiritual and corporal works of mercy are charitable actions by which we come to the aid of our neighbor in his spiritual and bodily necessities. Instructing, advising, consoling, and comforting are spiritual works of mercy, as are forgiving and patiently bearing wrongs. The corporal works of mercy consist especially in feeding the hungry sheltering the homeless, clothing the naked, visiting the sick and imprisoned, and burying the dead. Among all these, giving alms (money) to the poor is one of the chief witnesses to fraternal charity (brotherly love); it is also a work of justice pleasing to God (cf. Catechism of the Catholic Church Art 2447).

Ite missa est![189] This is normally understood to mean it is ended. But the literal translation of the words is "go *it* is *sent!*" Not *you* are sent! No. *It* is sent! The challenge for us then is to stop and ask ourselves: What is *it* that is sent? It is nothing less than what we have experienced through our participation in the Mass. ***The love of Christ as manifested in the words of the Scripture and sacrament.*** Thus, we must recognize that we don't just simply leave the Mass, as we would, for example, an opera or a ballgame. No! ***We are sent!*** We are sent by Christ Himself! To make His presence; His message; His love; and His person known to all we encounter after we have been sent. We are meant to make Him alive and relevant to those in whose presence we find ourselves. How? Simply put, we do this in the way we live our discipleship.[190] It is a challenge we are faced with by the dismissal as we leave the sacrifice of Calvary as re-presented in an unbloody manner upon the altar.

THE RECESSIONAL

And in anticipation of our being sent, the celebrating party formally recesses from the altar to symbolically "lead the way." Whether we find ourselves doing so actively, as did the Magdalene, or introspectively, as did the Blessed Mother, is no matter. What does, however, matter is that we do so in a way that the world in which we find ourselves is not only told but recognizes that "***He has risen!***"

---

[189] The following is taken from an article written by Knoblach, Tom Father. "Ite Missa Est." August 17, 2020, www.sacredheartsaukrapids.org

[190] The primary reason, for example, for the restoration of the diaconate to its proper place and function within the Church's hierarchy. To make Christ the Servant sacramentally present to the world in which he lives. LaDuca, Nicholas J. *Who Do You Say That I Am?* Amazon Press, 2021, p. 119.

CHAPTER SIX: CHALLENGES

The most important truth we can take away from His asking us to spend an hour with Him in the holy sacrifice of the Mass, is that it is ***an invitation***. Not a command, as He gave His apostles at the Last Supper to "do this in memory of me." Not an obligation[191] in the sense that one must obtain a driver's license to operate a car or a passport to travel abroad. No, it is more of an expectation on His part that we would want to do so. As, for example, an adult child to attend his parent's birthday party or visit one's grandparents on Christmas. It is something we know we should do and want to do.

Yet the invitation to do so offered by Jesus during His public ministry, when He wanted those who wished to have eternal life to eat His flesh and drink His blood was turned down by many then present. The same invitation He offers us now while seated at the right hand of His Father. To eat His glorified body and His resurrected blood.[192] An invitation that once again, sadly, I might add, is turned down by many of His disciples today.[193] Yet it is an invitation that was, is, and will continue to be offered until He comes again in His glory and that is His most ardent desire that we respond to. To spend one hour with us. What then holds us back? What is it that turns us away from spending that hour with Him?

I believe it can be traced directly to our understanding of the meaning of the hour. That the Mass is ***not*** merely a ritualistic exercise but a relational

---

[191] CCC 2042.

[192] It is interesting to note that both the Eastern Rite and Orthodox churches use heated wine to be consecrated to indicate it is the Resurrected Lord whose blood we consume. This is something I learned firsthand to my then surprise when at an Eastern Rite liturgy, I was presented with the chalice.

[193] Not merely our brothers and sisters of non-Catholic persuasions, but also Catholics, who in his discussion of the Eucharist, Bishop Barron points to a recent PEW report indicating that less than 25% of Catholics believe in the real presence as well.

experience. That it is ***not*** a performance we attend but an encounter that we enter into. An encounter that, to be truly meaningful, entails our full, conscious, and active participation[194] in the experience taking place. That the Mass is the means for our experiencing the sacrifice of Calvary first hand. That one recognizes it is because of that sacrifice we are presented in the consecrated species of bread and wine with the real presence of the Glorified Christ. The reality of which then challenges us to look at our disposition in not only approaching Him, but communing with Him in the Eucharist.

This reality that He is truly present causes us to face the realization that the Mass is a ***true sacrifice***. A sacrifice that we are invited to participate in by our presence at the holy sacrifice of the Mass. An invitation given us by the One who calls us His friends! An invitation that asks us to place ourselves at the scene. To place us along with the apostles at the Last Supper. To place ourselves on Calvary.

We must ask ourselves at the Mass, as the minsters proceed to the altar, can we put ourselves in the procession from the upper room, out the south gate, into the Garden of Gethsemane, to Capias' house, to the Praetorium, to the pillar on which He was scourged, to the cross and to the tomb? If not, why? As the ministers gather around the altar, can we put ourselves in the shoes of Mary, John, and the Magdalene and experience the sufferings and death of the One who, because of His love for us, willingly offered Himself to the Father for us? If not, why? As we receive the Eucharist, can we put ourselves in the place of Mary and receive Him as she did that day on Calvary? If not, why? As the Magdalene did on that Sunday morning, can we put ourselves in her stead and, after receiving the Risen Lord in the Eucharist, make haste to tell others of our experience? If not, why? As Peter, James, and John responded after their experience in Gethsemane by their witness to His command that we spend an hour with Him, can we too give our lives to His message, His promise, and His love as they did? If not, why?

---

[194] *Sacrosanctum Concilium* No. 14.

Therefore, to truly appreciate the meaning of His invitation to spend one hour with Him, we must first come to understand the Mass as a sacrifice. This is a challenge that was recognized by the Church in its demand that we consciously understand what we are doing when we attend Mass. By doing so, we will find ourselves more fully and actively contributing to what is taking place. In turn, this will bring us to a more aware realization of the real presence of the Glorified Lord in the Eucharist. This is a realization that will encourage us to look at our preparations to worthily receive Him in the Sacrament. An effort, that when the Mass ends, will enable us to go forth and truly make Him know to others by the way we live our discipleship.

FULL, ACTIVE, AND CONSCIOUS PARTICIPATION IN THE MASS

The first priority of the council fathers, as attested to in the first document promulgated, was to reform the liturgy.[195] This is a priority they identified would require those who participate in the liturgy to do so "fully, consciously, and actively."[196] It is a challenge given for one reason: that it is the "right and duty" of those participating to do so.[197] A "right and duty" that is still, for many, not completely understood. When challenged to "fully" participate in the Mass, many ask, "What does that involve?"[198] Giving our uninterrupted attention to the events unfolding? Giving our undivided devotion[199] to the hour we are asked to spend with Him? Or does it entail our giving unconditionally our whole personhood, body, mind, and spirit to live the experience of that Hour through our discipleship. This is an action that begins with our "active participation" in the Mass. In turn, this implies a "proactive" rather than reactive approach to our participation in the Mass. In other words, it implies a "missionary" approach that, to be effective, is really

---

[195] Sacrosanctum Concilium.

[196] Ibid. No 14.

[197] Ibid.

[198] An excellent discussion of this challenge is given in an article written by Colleen Campbell. "Full, Active, Conscious: Liturgy and Life." Catholicapostoltecenter.org, March 20, 2020.

[199] EP I.

a commitment. It is a commitment to approach Christ not only in the Mass, where we encounter Him in His Word and in His Sacrament, but in the world that we reenter when we leave the Mass. Whether that encounter is expected or not. Whether those we encounter are among the "good, the wicked, or the unpleasant." Whether they are believers or not. This is a challenge requiring us to be "conscious" of what our participation in the Mass entails. A consciousness of what is involved in the responses we give to what it is He is offering us in His Word we hear and in His Sacrament we receive. And because we accept His offerings, we must be conscious of the consequences those gifts will have on our living our discipleship. A consciousness of our need, once we leave the Mass, to live His new commandment.[200] A consciousness of the path offered to us as His disciples and the efforts needed on our part to walk that path. A consciousness that will enable us to recognize not only God's presence, but His desire that we offer our lives to Him, as He did His life to His Father—*unconditionally*. The challenge for us is to ask ourselves, are we ready to do so?

THE MASS AS A TRUE SACRIFICE

From apostolic times, the Mass has been accepted as, believed to be, and celebrated as a *sacrifice*. Yet when faced with the reality that the Mass is a true sacrifice, we find it difficult to form a clear conception of what that means. This is a challenge that has, and still does, create difficulties for not only our Protestant brethren, but also, sadly, members of our Catholic family, as well as many theologians who have both studied and written on the subject.[201] Muller says that the Mass is "a subject so grand and so sublime" that it is "incomprehensible to human reason."[202] Yet the theme of sacrifice takes us to the heart of the Gospel and the

---

[200] John 13:34-35.

[201] Yet as Jason Evert points out, of all the Catholic doctrines that that are denigrated as unbiblical, the sacrifice of the Mass has perhaps the most scriptural evidence that both non-Catholics *and* Catholics are aware of. Evert, Jason. "Is the Mass a Sacrifice?" *The Mystery Box*, September 1, 2001.

[202] Muller, Michael, Fr. *The Holy Sacrifice of the Mass*. Tan Books Rockford, Illinois, 1992, p. 13.

essence of the Christian faith. In a very real sense, "the theme of sacrifice constitutes Christianity."[203]

Therefore, it is imperative we understand what it means when we affirm that the Mass is a ***true sacrifice***. Because as the author of the Letter to the Hebrews declares, ***"Christ's sacrifice was offered only once"*** (cf. 9:6-7; 10:1) ***"and accepted in heaven"*** (cf. 8:2,5). Because, as Catholics, we are going to be challenged as to why it is we can say the Mass is a sacrifice? We will be asked if what we do in the Mass is not merely a repeating of the one and accepted sacrifice? And our answer is No! It is not a repeating of, but ***a re-presentation of the same sacrifice***. Is it another sacrifice? Again, our answer must be No! Why? Because it is ***the same sacrifice, albeit in an unbloody manner***. Or as the Catechism explains, "[I]n the divine sacrifice which is celebrated in the Mass, ***the same Christ who offered Himself once in a bloody manner on the altar of the cross is contained and offered in an unbloody manner***" (emphasis added).[204]

This is a sacrifice that is re-presented in a way that the one, perfect, and unrepeatable sacrifice of the cross is ***perpetuated in the sacrifice of the Mass***.[205] The Mass, in which the Eucharistic sacrifice is offered, but "only in union with Christ's all-sufficient Sacrifice on Calvary." If it were not, Shamon continues, "the Eucharist would have as much or as little value as its Old Testament prototypes seen in the sacrifices of Abel, Abraham, and Melchizedek."[206] But by attesting four times during the Liturgy of the Eucharist, we proclaim that it is![207] A sacrifice that is perpetuated in the Mass.[208] A sacrifice that occurred some 2000 years ago on Calvary and which, through the Mass, is made a permanent piece of heaven.[209]

---

[203] Zaspel, Fred. *The Theology of Sacrifice*. The Gospel Coalition.

[204] CCC NO 1367.

[205] Oury, Guy, Rev. *The Mass*. Catholic Book Publishing Company, New York, 1988, p. 105.

[206] Shamon, Albert Joseph Mary, Rev. *Behind the Mass*. The Riehle Foundation, Milford, Ohio, 1995, p. 60.

[207] Lustier, Jean Marie, Cardinal. *The Mass*. Harper and Row, San Francisco, 1987, p. 52. Lustier identifies the four times as in the opening dialogue, the mystery of faith, the fraction, and at the end in the doxology.

[208] Oury, p. 105.

[209] Driscoll, Jeremy, OSB. *What Happens at Mass*. Gracewing Publishing, 2005, p. 81.

The Mass, the hour, His hour, the hour by which He begins through His passion, experiences through His cross, overcomes through His resurrection, and accomplishes through His ascension. The hour He asks of us to spend with Him, which is more than a mere "event." It is an experience, an encounter, that does not pass away. Why? Because it is a reality that transcends time. It is a reality that not only does the Risen and Glorified God come to us through the Mass, but more importantly, it is through the Mass that we can come to Him most perfectly in the Eucharist. It is the hour in which the mysterious and miraculous reality that comes into existence through the words of consecration said by the priest over a piece of unleavened[210] wheat bread and a chalice of wine from the grape happens. The hour during which, by the words given through the command of Our Lord at the Last Supper to "do this," enable us to be present at the re-presentation of the sacrifice on Calvary.

Yet by definition, when one gets right down to it, a sacrifice is nothing more (or less) than a means of giving something up. So then, if at the Mass, in defiance of all that has been written, practiced, and proclaimed, it is *not* Our Lord who is "given up" for the many, then who or what is? When the priest, using the words of consecration given to us by Jesus Himself, holds up the bread and says, "This is my body which will be *given up* for you," what is he saying? That it is merely "symbolic" and that it is really the wheat, sacrificed by the farmer who reaped it to "give up" to the baker? Or is it really the bread that the baker "gives up" to the consumer? That makes no sense. The same could be said for the wine, which is "shed" (given) for the many. Is it the grape "given up" by the grower to the brewer? Or the wine "given up" to the retailer? Again, ridiculous!

Stop and think about that. When the priest holds up the consecrated bread or the minister presents us with that same bread, what do we, the Church, *and others* refer to it as? Not "the bread" but *the Host!* This is a term derived from Latin "hostia," meaning **victim or sacrifice.**[211] Thus, as we approach the Host and before we receive the Host, which is

---

[210] Albeit our brethren of the Orthodox and Eastern Rites used leavened bread to confect the true sacrifice by which the Eucharist is made present.

[211] https://ask.library.harvard.edu.

presented us by the minister as the *"Body of Christ"*—we are challenged to ask ourselves, in terms of our acclamation, our Amen, what are we saying yes to? A symbolic piece of bread *or* the glorified body, blood, soul and divinity of the Risen Lord? The One who comes to us in the reality of the Eucharist, through and only through *the sacrifice of the Mass*. The *same sacrifice* once and for all time offered up so perfectly by Our Lord on the cross of Calvary but *now re-presented*.

THE REAL PRESENCE

As a matter of faith, Catholics have always held that through the words of consecration spoken by the priest *in persona christi*, Jesus becomes sacramentally and mysteriously really present. Under the appearances of bread and wine, the glorified body, blood, soul and divinity of Christ is truly present. This is a belief that has basically been unanimously held for the first 1500 years of the Church's existence. A belief that didn't come to be doubted and even denied in earnest until the advent of the Protestant Reformation.[212] An essential belief that I contend defines Catholicism.

Yet this truth is not merely a belief: it is a reality. A truth that has its genesis not in any Church teaching or theological precept but in the words of Jesus Himself! Words we hear proclaimed in the Gospels of Matthew,[213] Mark,[214] and Luke,[215] as well in Saint Paul's first letter to the Corinthians.[216] That the bread He broke and gave them was His body; that the chalice containing the wine was His blood. Furthermore, He told them they were not only to eat the bread which was His body and drink the wine which was His blood. No! *They were to continue to do so in remembrance of Him*.

---

[212] 2019 Pew Research Center's American Trends Panel Wave 44 Final Topline February 4-19, 2019. In this report, the results showed that 31% believed the bread and wine became the body and blood of Jesus Christ, while 69% believed the bread and wine are symbols of the body and blood of Jesus Christ.

[213] Matthew 26:17-29.

[214] Mark 14:12-25.

[215] Luke 22:7-38.

[216] 1 Corinthians 11:23-25.

This is a reality by which He provided those who believe the means for achieving what He promised at His bread of life discourse: eternal life![217] A discourse where He revealed that the means of attaining eternal life is by eating His flesh and drinking His blood, which He says not once, but some six times to reiterate this truth. What I find of interest is that those who refute or deny this truth by declaring these words to be merely "symbolic" are quick to take other Scripture passages as literal in their efforts to refute Catholic teachings.[218] A position, in reference to the real presence, that is neither Scriptural based,[219] apostolically based,[220] patristically based,[221] or theologically supportable.[222]

This is an interpretation that provides a sense of "rationalization" that allows them to say the Mass, therefore, is not a true sacrifice because the same Lord, albeit in His risen and glorified body, is not really present. A position that then leads one to perceive the Mass as merely a memorial or a voluntary gathering of Christians. An understanding, therefore, that should be left to the person to decide whether or not to attend rather than find it to be a response to the One who is asking us to do so. The One whose hour it is. The One who is asking us whether or not we believe enough in His Presence to spend that hour with Him. The One who is asking us to participate in His one and perfect sacrifice. The One who offers us that unmerited privilege through the holy sacrifice of the Mass. The One who is truly and really present in a more perfect way in the Eucharist. The question is not can we, for we can! But *will we*?

CAN YOU SPEND ONE HOUR WITH ME

Now, we come face to face with the challenge that began our journey. The challenge to spend His hour with Him. The hour that the Father

---

[217] John 6:22-57.

[218] E.g., The references to Jesus' "brothers" and "sisters" in refuting the Church's teachings on the Ever-virgin Mary.

[219] E.g., John 51, 53, 54, 55, 56, 57.

[220] E.g., 1 Cor 11:23.

[221] Origen, *Homilies on Numbers* 7:2 (A.D. 248)

[222] Augustine, *Explanations of the Psalms* 33:1:10 (A.D. 405); Saint Thomas Aquinas Question 75, Article 4, *Summa Theologica*.

deemed from the beginning to be the means of His family's redemption. The hour the Son willingly and obediently but more so out of love accepted unconditionally. The hour by which He challenged not only us, who call ourselves His disciples, but all of mankind to enter into so as to experience through His passion, death, resurrection, and ascension the depth of His love for us. The hour by which we, who say yes to Him, will find ourselves transcending time.[223] Where we will not only experience what took place some 2000 years ago but have a foretaste of what we will experience in the future. An hour not only that He wishes us to share with Him but the hour that He earnestly desires to share with us (Luke 22:14). A desire by which He is letting us know that it is His wish that we do so not merely as an obligation (although, if we want to be His disciples, we also must take up our cross daily; Luke 9:23). That we do so not merely as a challenge, even though if we wish to share in eternal life, we are challenged by Him to eat His flesh and drink His blood (John 6:26-71). No, we are challenged to do so as a demonstration of how much we love Him (John 13:30). How much we desire to share in His life (John 17:21). To show, by our willingness to share in His hour, how much we desire to sit with Him at His Father's table in heaven (John 14:3). This is the hour that brings us to the culmination of the mystery of salvation. The hour that can be summed up in one word: **love**.[224]

The hour that we are challenged to personally experience. The hour we are challenged to participate in fully, actively, and consciously. The hour we are challenged to embrace in a way that through our discipleship, the fruits of His hour will be experienced by all the world.

Yet, Our Lord, though He does not compel us to do anything we choose not to do, does desire that we do spend His hour with Him. His request is like a request we receive to attend a friend's birthday party, to attend opera, or to follow a particular path of discipleship, whether it be as an ordained minister, a member of a religious order, or by living the

---

[223] Guardini, Romano. *Meditations before Mass.* Sophia Institute Press, Manchester, New Hampshire, 1955, p. 67.
[224] Howard, Thomas. *If Your Mind Wanders at Mass.* Ignatius Press, San Francisco, 2001, p. 103.

Sacrament of Marriage. However, no matter how it is that we are asked by Him to share the fruits of His hour, one thing is required to do so: our response to His request. A response that can be an outright refusal (as the disciples did in response to His bread of life discourse [cf. John 6:60]), or a maybe it is conditional (like the one who wanted to first bury his parents [cf. Luke 9:59]), or as Our Lord who is inviting us desires, *an unqualified yes* (as Peter responded to Our Lord's command to "eat His flesh and drink His blood" [John 6:68]).

This is a response by which we need the courage of our faith in the One asking us to spend His hour with Him to say, "Yes, Lord! Not only can I, but *I will* spend an hour with you. I will spend an hour with you, *'fully, actively, and consciously'* in the holy sacrifice of the Mass." Because if our faith and devotion (EP I) are truly up to it, then by spending an hour with Him in the holy sacrifice of the Mass, "we will find, every time we do so, a true encounter with the Risen Lord Jesus Christ."[225]

---

[225] Dubruiel, Michael. *The How-to Book of the Mass.* Our Sunday Visitor Huntington, Indiana, 2002, p. 18.

CHAPTER SEVEN: CONCLUSION

After having read, researched, and reflected on what I would call a mere "speck" of what has been written and said about it,[226] the Mass can be summed up as nothing other than a **love story**. Not any love story, mind you, but an intimate, mysterious, never-ending story of God's love for us. It is the Father's love for us as manifested in His gift to us of His Son. The Son's love for us as manifested in His incarnation, by which that love was evidenced most perfectly in His passion, death, resurrection, and ascension. The Holy Spirit's love for us in becoming one with us through our baptism. A love manifested in His taking the Son's, as well as our, sacrifice, as offered in the Mass to the Father in a way that is accepted once and for all eternity.

It is a love that is revealed to us through the proclamation of the Gospel by the deacon, by which He reveals why, out of love, He did what He did for us. A love that is not only received, but entered into by those present through the Sacrament of the Eucharist. A love that is recognized by the acclamation of those present affirming what He, out of love for us, has done.

It is a never-ending love story that began at the Last Supper, when by that love, He offered us His body, under the appearances of bread, and His blood, under the appearances of wine, as the means for us to attain eternal life. A continuing love affair that is experienced in a real and intimate way through the holy sacrifice of the Mass. A never-ending love affair that will be experienced for all eternity around the Father's banquet table in heaven. It is a love affair that is made possible for us to experience through the words of consecration, by which He reveals what He, by His love for us, has willingly done for us because of that love.

Reflecting on the holy sacrifice of the Mass as I have done, I find that my experiences as a deacon provide me with a unique perspective. *Not*

---

[226] See, for example, the Selected Bibliography.

participating as does the priest, who through the words of consecration re-presents the **same** perfect and unrepeatable sacrifice in an unbloody manner; **nor** as the lay congregation, who participate in the Mass through their prayers, gestures, and responses in a fully active and conscious way; but as I think of myself as the "table master,"[227] the "Maître d." Put differently, as the one who can be identified as a "bridge" between the priest, who acting **in persona christi**, offers us the gift of eternal life, and the recipients, those participating in the Mass as the Body of Christ, who are there to receive the gift of eternal life.

For it is the deacon who, like the Roman soldier at Calvary, prepares the place on Golgotha/the altar where the crucifixion/sacrifice will take place. Who, in laying down the cross/corporal on which the victim will be laid, anticipates the sacrifice that will take place. Who, like the soldier, places the victim's body on the cross/corporal under the species of bread and wine. Who, by lifting up the crucified one/chalice, shows all that the sacrifice has been accomplished. Who, in presenting His body/the Host to those present, as did the Roman soldier to His mother that Friday 2000 years ago. Who dismisses those present who had witnessed the crucifixion/Holy Sacrifice of the Mass, as did the Roman soldiers, to go back to where they came from and share not the end of the story, but its eternal continuation through their witness.

And it is in this dismissal, whether priest celebrant, deacon server, or lay participant, that all are challenged to pause and reflect on the "faith and devotion" by which we participated in the Mass. We can see whether we found ourselves to be "passersby," distant observers, or standing at the foot of the cross, asking ourselves, "Where were we when they crucified my Lord?" From my perspective, standing at the side of the priest, I find myself close to the cross, identifying more with the Magdalene. And in that experience, I find I am given another lesson from the love story I just participated in. A lesson from which I believe all who choose to spend an hour with Him in the Mass can learn of what His love means for us as His disciples. Now, why the Magdalene? Why not Mary, the sinless one? Or John, the beloved one? Because like the Magdalene,

---

[227] Acts:6-4.

standing at the altar of sacrifice, I, too, recognize not only what my sins contributed to, but more importantly, what His sacrifice has brought me: His forgiveness.

Now, while the Blessed Mother, sinless from the moment of her conception, is the model, the ideal to which we all, as disciples of her Son, aspire to be like, it is an aspiration that we will only achieve in heaven. And although most Christians desire to respond to her challenge to do what He tells us, which here is to spend an hour with Him in the Mass, I find, realistically, that we often fail to meet that mark. John, for example, who is recognized as Jesus' beloved, and in faith I believe that we too are loved by Jesus as He loved John, who spent an Hour with Him. Yet I know that, for whatever reason, we often find ourselves drifting apart from the bosom of Jesus, from His hour, the Mass, where we like John, will find Him offering us Himself as well.

Yet in the Magdalene, I find, particularly as a deacon, comfort in the fact that she did nothing but serve Him; anoint Him; and follow Him. Not only to the cross and to witness His crucifixion; but to the tomb in which He was laid. And as I find myself preparing to receive Him in the Eucharist, to understand better what Our Lord told her in the garden where His tomb was that first Easter Sunday morning, when He said to her don't touch me, "I have not ascended to my Father" (cf. John 20:17). In other words, what He is saying to us is that the bread and the wine which will be offered up for us has not yet been consecrated. That it is not the crucified body, but the glorified body that will be offered to us as the means for obtaining everlasting life. The body that was crucified and killed and now has risen that will be glorified when He stands at the right hand of the Father. The body that is presented to us by the minister of Holy Communion through the words "the Body of Christ."

The faith in Him that enables us, as it did her to hear Him, that He will come to us in the Host, as He did her in the garden, and in doing so, embrace us, as He did John, and provide us the means to be like Mary when, through eating His body and drinking His blood, we will have the means to experience eternal life. A life in which we, like Mary, will know no sin. A life that will enable us, as she did, to unconditionally say to her Son, "Let it be done to me, according to your Word."

For it is in and through our communion with Him that we will find not only the confidence to, but the graces by which, to walk not merely with Him, but before Him (cf. Matthew 28:19-20). We can have the clarity to see that we not merely *on* a mission: we *are* God's mission. The mission of living our discipleship in a way that tells the world all that He said and did. A mission that we can only achieve by having the courage of our faith to *spend one hour with Him*! How? By our full, active, and conscious participation in the holy sacrifice of the Mass.

CHAPTER EIGHT: EPILOGUE

In undertaking this work, I have found the sources referencing the Mass to be vast. The scope unbounded. The depth unfathomable. Whether it be that of an apostolic father, a renown theologian, a saint, or a modern evangelist, a study of their works on the Mass[228] reveals that the reality of the Mass is unfathomable to the human intellect. The fullness of which can only be truly understood; truly experienced; and truly entered into by having faith in Him, whose perfect sacrifice we are privileged to witness re-presented in an unbloody manner. A faith that enables us to say yes to His desire that we spend one hour with Him. A faith that enables us to believe the truth that He is really present under the appearances of the bread and wine, which through the words of consecration became, in essence, His body, blood, soul, and divinity. A faith that enables us to see that the Mass "is the moment when we, as individuals and as community join with God, really, actually realistically, and truly."[229] A faith in His promise that by receiving the Eucharist, by which we eat His body and drink His blood sacramentally, we will have "life eternal."

But it is also the faith necessary to realize that although the deacon proclaims "the Mass is ended," *it is not over*. If we listen closely, we find we are not being dismissed, as we might at the end of a class or dance recital. No! We are being *sent*! Sent as we hear to *"glorify Him"* not in an ecclesial or communal way, but in a personal way by our words, our actions, and our deeds as we live our lives in the world in which we work, play, and live. We are sent to proclaim the *"good news,"* again by living our discipleship in a way that Christ's presence, Christ's love, and Christ's encouragement is experienced by those we encounter.

But for us to be able to do so, the Church tells us that it is necessary that we not only *come to* **the Mass but that we** *go from the Mass with proper*

---

228 As seen in the Selected Bibliography, which is, in reality, a drop in the bucket as to the scope and depth of written works available on the Mass.

229 Brieg, James. *Why Go to Mass?* Liguori Publications, Liguori, Missouri, 1978, p. 10.

dispositions. Coming to Mass with the right disposition, we are told, will not only enable us, but encourage us to recognize that the Mass is "something more" than the mere observation of the laws governing [its] valid and licit celebration.[230] We come to realize that the Mass is not a "ritualistic exercise" but a "relational experience." An experience by which we encounter God, here in the Person of the Glorified Christ, in a unique and personal way.[231] It is something that we can only come to realize through our "full, conscious and active participation in the liturgy," which the Church reminds us "is the primary and indispensable source from which the faithful are to derive the true Christian spirit"[232]

The Spirit to "go!"

To go from the congregation that gathered to offer, along with the priest celebrant the sacrifice that the Father would find acceptable. To go and share the good news as proclaimed in the Scriptures unveiled in the Liturgy of the Word. To go and share the experience of being there to witness sacramentally the re-presentation of the sacrifice of the cross. To go—and with the blessings given at the conclusion of the liturgy—live what was heard and what was experienced in a way that all will know the Christ who died for us, is risen, has ascended into heaven, and, as promised, will be with us always.

In His body, the Church; in its members, whether clergy, religious, or laity who have in common their baptism; in His Sacraments, which will enable all, from the beginning of life to its consummation, to "Live Jesus!" But most of all, in His love, which He, along with His Father, gives us in the Holy Spirit.

All in all, this only happens if we but have the courage to spend ***"one hour with Him."*** An "hour" that transcends time. An "hour" that allows us a foretaste what awaits us in heaven. An "hour" that He tells us he ***desires*** to spend with us. The hour that He first asked Peter, James, and John in the Garden of Gethsemane to spend with Him. The hour He

---

[230] *Sacrosanctum Concilium* No. 11.

[231] Fushek, Dale Fr, and Dodds, Bill. *Your One-Stop Guide to The Mass.* Servant Publications, Ann Arbor, Michigan, 2000, p. 7.

[232] *Sacrosanctum Concilium* No. 14.

is asking of us to spend with Him. The hour we are asked to not only spend with Him, but *share with Him; enter into with Him; experience with Him.* The hour that is known to us as the holy sacrifice of the Mass.

The challenge for us is not can we, but will we spend that hour with Him? Do we truly desire to spend one hour with Him in the Mass to learn how the story ends? What better way to show that by daring to spend an Hour with Him we expose ourselves to the graces one needs to deal with any challenge of faith we may be exposed to, than by a personal experience. An experience by which I learned firsthand in my discernment at the end of my formation, to ask my bishop to ordain me to the Order of Deacon. A challenge I found no better way to face than to take Him up on His offer to spend an Hour with Him. Which I did by attending Mass one Saturday in the chapel of a Jesuit retreat house. In preparing to spend that Hour with Him at Mass, I asked the Lord to help me discern my call to the diaconate. At the end of the Mass, I found myself responding to a man's request to "tie his shoes". While kneeling down before him and tying his shoes, I heard Our Lord telling me that He too, as a servant, knelt down to wash His disciple's feet (using the Greek the word to describe what He did as *diakonia*). That He came in His humanity to serve me. Would I, in turn, have the confidence to serve Him as a deacon? And because of that experience I found the confidence to say to Him, in my response to my bishop, some forty years ago, "Yes, Lord, I will serve you. Yes Lord, not only will I spend an Hour with You, but I will do so as your servant." The same experience we will have, if we but have the courage to say, "Yes, Lord, I will! I will spend this Hour with You in the Mass." For by doing so, we too *will see firsthand*, as I did that day some forty years ago, kneeling before my bishop, how the story ends.[233]

---

[233] Fushek, Dale Fr, and Dodds, Bill. *Your One-Stop Guide to The Mass.* Servant Publications, Ann Arbor, Michigan, 2000, p. 10.

Selected Bibliography

______________. "The Mass—Parts of the Mass." http: churchof htesacredheart.org/faith

Belmonte, Charles. *Understanding the Mass.* Scepter Publications, Princeton, New Jersey, 1997.

Brieg, James. *Why Go to Mass?* Liguori Publications, Liguori, Missouri, 1978.

Buono, Anthony M. *Active Participation at Mass.* Alb House, New York, 1994.

Carstens, Christopher. *A Devotional Journey into the Mass.* Sophia Institute Manchester, New Hampshire, 2017.

Champlin, Joseph M. *The Mystery and Meaning of the Mass.* The Crossword Publishing Company, New York, 1998.

Dalmais, Irenee Henri, Gy, Pierre Marie, Jounel, Pierre, and Martimort, Aime Georges. *The Church at Prayer Volume I Principles of the Liturgy.* The Liturgical Press, 1987.

Daniel-Rops, Henri. *This is the Mass,* translated by Alastair Guinan. Hawthorne Books, Inc., New York, 1959.

Driscoll, Jeremy, OSB. *What Happens at Mass.* Gracewing Publishing, Herefordshire HR6 0QF, England. 2005.

Dubruiel, Michael. *The How-To Book of the Mass.* Our Sunday Visitor Huntington, Indiana, 2002.

Fisher, Eugene J Ed. *The Jewish Roots of Christian Liturgy.* Paulist Press, New York/Mahwah, 1990.

Fushek, Dale Fr, and Dodds, Bill. *Your One-Stop Guide to the Mass.* Servant Publications, Ann Arbor, Michigan, 2000.

Guardini, Romano. *Meditations before Mass.* Sophia Institute Press, Manchester, New Hampshire, 1955.

Hahn, Scott, and Flaherty, Regis J. *Catholic for a Reason III.* Emmaus Road Steubenville, Ohio, 2004.

Hahn, Scott. *The Lamb's Supper: The Mass as Heaven and Earth.* Doubleday, 1999.

Howard, Thomas. *If Your Mind Wanders at Mass.* Ignatius Press, San Francisco, 2001.

Irwin, Kevin W. *Response to 101 Questions on the Mass.* Paulist Press, New York/Mahwah, New Jersey, 1999.

Irwin, Kevin W. Msgr. (Author), David Lysik (Editor) The *Liturgy Documents, Volume One, Fourth Edition.* Liturgy Training Publications, Archdiocese of Chicago, 2004.

__________. *The Liturgy Documents, Volume Two.* Liturgy Training Publications, Archdiocese of Chicago, 1999.

Johnson J., Lawrence. *The Mystery of Faith: A Study of the Structural Elements of the Mass.* Federation of Diocesan Liturgical Commissions, Revised Edition, 2003.

Jungmann, Joseph A. S. J. *The Mass of the Roman Rite: Its Origins and Development.* Christian Classics, Inc., Westminster, Maryland, 1992.

Likoudis, James, and Whitehead, Kenneth D. *The Pope, The Council, and the Mass: Answers to the Questions the "Traditionalists" Have Asked.* Emmaus Road Steubenville, Ohio, 2003.

Lustier, Jean Marie, Cardinal. *The Mass.* Harper and Row, San Francisco, 1987.

McGuckian, Michael, S. J. *The Holy Sacrifice of the Mass.* Hillenbrand Books, Chicago, Illinois, 2005.

Meagher, James L., Fr. *How Christ Said the First Mass.* Tan Books, Rockford, Illinois, 1984.

Muller, Michael, Fr. *The Holy Sacrifice of the Mass*. Tan Books, Rockford, Illinois, 1992.

Nash, Thomas J. *The Biblical Roots of the Mass*. Sophia Institute Press, Manchester, New Hampshire, 2015.

Nichols, Aidan, O. P. *Looking at the Liturgy: A Critical View of its Contemporary Form*. Ignatius Press, San Francisco, 1996.

Oury, Guy, Rev. *The Mass*. Catholic Book Publishing Company, New York, 1988.

Pitre, Brant. *Jesus and the Jewish Roots of the Eucharist: Unlocking the Secrets of the Last Supper*. Image, New York, 2016.

Ratzinger, Joseph Cardinal. *The Spirit of the Liturgy*. Ignatius Press, San Francisco, 2000.

Roguet, A. M. Rev OP. *The New Mass*. Catholic Book Publishing Company, New York, 1970.

Shamon, Albert Joseph Mary, Rev. *Behind the Mass*. The Riehle Foundation, Milford, Ohio, 1995.

Stravinskas, Peter, Rev. *The Bible and the Mass*. Newman House Press, Mount Pocono, Pennsylvania, 2000.

Trigilio, Jr., John Rev., Brighenti, Kenneth Rev., and Cafone, James Rev Monsignor. *Catholic Mass for Dummies*. Wiley Publishing, Hoboken, New Jersey, 2011.

Trenham, Josiah Fr. "Preparing Yourself for Liturgy." http: churchof htesacredheart.org/faith.

Von Cochem, Martin Fr. *The Incredible Catholic Mass*. Tan Books, Charlotte, North Carolina, 2012.

Walsh, Eugene A., S. S. *The Order of the Mass: Guidelines*. Pastoral Arts Associates of North America, Glendale, Arizona, 1979.

Wuerl, Donald Cardinal. *The Mass*. Doubleday, New York, 2011.